RESTORE
THE
JOY

RESTORE
THE
JOY

A Transformation Through Confirmation

DR. LAURA COLSON

Copy editor © Andrea C. Jasmin
www.acjasminproofreading.com
Front and back cover design © Amber Edwards
www.theedwardsproject.com
Interior book design © Melissa Clampitt
www.melissaclampittdesigns.com

Back cover photo © Michael Maxwell Photography
www.michaelmaxwellphotography.com

To contact the publisher, visit
info@mybigegolife.com
To contact author, visit
info@mybigegolife.com

ISBN 978-1-7328961-3-0

Printed in the United States of America

DEDICATION

To my dad, Calvin Monrae Colson, Sr.

Written June 5, 2019 at 10:48 a.m. (graveside on your birthday) I have not been to visit you since March 3rd. That was a day that I will never forget. I almost feel as if you have passed on a sixth sense to me as God continues to move in me and give me confirmation of things I have prayed and ask Him to REveal. A lot has taken place since that time. I am settling into my new home, the other house was placed on the market and sold in less time than I could imagine considering its state. A medical diagnosis has me taking a prescription daily, and my divorce process is almost complete. Who would have ever imagined I would be going through four of the five most stressful life events all at one time? And who would have thought that I would be strong enough to endure it all?

I used to joke about you always referencing Romans 10:9 (NIV), "If you declare with your mouth, Jesus is Lord, and believe in your heart that God raised him from the dead, you will be saved, I now REalize the importance of REpetition and speaking about faith consistently as I study the Word intentionally first thing in the morning and throughout the day.

Sunday mornings have become bittersweet for me. I anticipate worship but a melancholy feeling comes over me as I expect to hear your resounding "YEAH." As a child I would feel ashamed and wouldn't focus on the message because I was so focused on you. But oh, to be able to hear your voice and have you in my presence again.

I also REcall you carrying around a rock in your pocket, and when we went to a store you would empty out your pocket looking for the correct change. And as a REsult, people would ask why you had that rock. You would respond, "He without sin cast the first stone, and I can't cast it!" (John 8:7 American Standard Version).

With all that I have and continue to go through, and as much as your personal praise and testimony would embarrass me in my younger life, I now REalize what it means when the old gospel song says, "We'll understand it better by and by."

Your spirit lives within me. You always talked about how someone was going to preach, and you focused on Calvin, Jr. so much, but I think the ministry may be in me. God has been truly moving in my life, but my walk with Him became different when I REalized that your days with us on this earth were coming to an end. I became very intentional about my faith walk, and I strive to be a willing vessel for others to come to know Him. I may not stand in a pulpit on Sunday mornings, but I am committed to using various platforms to share the goodness of our Lord and Savior, Jesus Christ. I pray that my book will be one way for His word to be REceived. As a quote REminds me, my life may be the only Bible some will ever REad. I'm just trying to be a vessel so others may be able to REceive Him. Unbeknownst to you, I hit rock bottom December 2017. I knew the Lord before because of you and mom, but I had to truly get to know Him for myself these past few years. My life has forever changed since then. I'm striving to be authentic so others know that He doesn't expect for us to be perfect, but progress and praise Him in all things

Thank you, dah, for who you were for me and for many others. You will forever live on in my heart and continue to inspire me to spread the word and most importantly, love, of Jesus. ~11:37 a.m.

My dad has truly become my guardian angel. I know he is watching over me and I can sense him as I navigate life. In the same manner that he was a blessing to my life, I hope that this book may be used to spread the news about God's goodness, grace, mercy, and REstoration of my life to help others along the way, just as my dad shared his personal testimonies with others during his life.

CONTENTS

FOREWORD

She went through the fire and she went through the rain
She fought, she cried to mask her pain
I saw the tears I watched the misery,
And now the world is witnessing herstory

I sat on the front row; I saw it all
I saw when she slipped, but God caught her fall
Painful to watch, but I was there for a reason
Right by her side, through all of her seasons

From separation, divorce, illness, death and financial distress
Insecurity, heartbreak, loss, even pains in her chest
Her eyes were sad, her spirit broken
The enemy tried to steal her joy

I held the phone when all she spoke were moans,
But the Holy Spirit translated to the Father all of her sorrow and her groans
For hours at a time, I listened to her release
Watching her transform has been inspiring to say the least

The great Ephesians and Romans were her tour guides
Joel, TD, Keion and Steven became her closest guys
The Circle Maker and *Return to Love* were her anchors
"Life and Favor" and "Blessings in the Storm" were her saviors

RESTORE THE JOY

Three little souls needing her to be strong,
They needed their mother's love as they were hurting too
Little did she know that it wouldn't be long,
Until she experienced her own BreakT.H.R.O.U.G.H.

But one day, seemed like overnight,
She became even stronger from the fight
The joy of the Lord gave her peace
She got up off her knees and the storms calmed and ceased

She realized that God's love alone is sustainable
Pain to purpose, trials to triumph, mess into a message,
And now she is uncontainable

She created vision boards, sold meals, oils, jewels,
And now, a book
This is how a Godly transformation looks
You called me your miracle and while I understand why
It was really God working through me, from the tears that I too once cried

The wait was over
The weight came off
Head held high, chin up when she walked
She began inspiring other lives as she coached and talked

You went through the fire and you went through the rain
You fought, you cried to mask your pain
I saw the tears; I watched the misery,
And now the world is witnessing your story

The story of how you REstored the joy

-MH (a.k.a. Miracle Michelle)

ACKNOWLEDGEMENTS

I must begin my acknowledgements as tradition in the black church; I must first give honor to God—My Lord and Savior who is truly the center of my life—for everything He ordains. None of this would have been possible without the plan He had in store for me. To Dr. Clifford A. Jones, Sr. (and First Lady C. Brenda Jones), my pastor at Friendship Missionary Baptist Church in Charlotte, North Carolina, who (now in the absence of my father) serves as my adoptive father, I thank you for your leadership, guidance, and treating me as one of your own. From the time our family joined the church and I was baptized in 1985, up until now, helping me through some of the toughest times in my adulthood.

As I work to gather my thoughts of how to truly express my gratitude and appreciation to the one who gave me life, tears have filled in my eyes. To you, Phadiona Colson, the one God chose specifically to love and nurture me before I ever took my first breath, words cannot begin to express the gratitude and appreciation for all that you have done and continue to do in my life. Though I can never say it enough, you are the reason that I am so compassionate, caring, and nurturing; for you led by example. The story that is revealed here speaks to the strength I developed by working to emulate you.

Who would have ever thought that I would grow to be so close to my brother? As a little girl, I thought you hated me, Calvin, because of the way you would beat me up and try to torture me, but I see now that all of those struggles contributed to me being the strong and resilient woman I am today. Thank you for calling me out in 2017 and for realizing that I was going through something. I appreciate you encouraging me to do what I needed to do for myself and reminding me to not worry about what others had to say. Though dad has transitioned, he truly continues to live on in my life through you.

Dominic, Morgan, and Mason, life would not be worth living without you. You are my heartbeats, you are my why, and I love you more than words can express.

Uncle K and Aunt Linda, thank you both for the roles you played in my life—knowingly and unknowingly. I have learned a lot from your lives, your commitment to work, and dedication to your families, but most importantly to yourselves.

Michelle Williams, Miracle Michelle, my big siSTAR, my circle maker friend, prayer warrior, the one who literally sat on the phone and truly was (and continues to be) a listening ear when I couldn't even develop the words to speak many a days and nights. As I always say, Everything God Ordains. I am grateful that the Lord allowed our paths to cross on the campus of Johnson C. Smith University as I walked down the hall when you first arrived on campus, and I yelled out, "I smell vinegar!" As I peered into your office and you looked at me like, "Who in the world is this loud woman?" we would make a connection as UNC alums. During our first lunch outing at Angie's Diner on "The Ford," we both committed to "keep it real" with one another about everything (even though those chicken wings we were eating were unrealistic in size—LOL) . . . and you have stayed true to that. Though we went our separate ways for a few years navigating life as wives, mothers, and professionals, it was all a part of His master plan to bring us full circle, not knowing that He had prepared you to help me go T.H.R.O.U.G.H. to get to my breakthrough. You have helped me draw closer to our Father. From you encouraging me to read *The Power of I Am* by Joel Osteen, to rising with me EVERY morning for the past few years now to share God's word and encouraging messages through an app, to our personal praise and worship sessions and concerts as we prepare for each day—whether preparing for battle or claiming the victory—from Cheez-Its to personal DoorDash Cookout deliveries, to new and healthy beginnings, we now look back and can see we are living our latter and our best is yet to come, for we haven't seen nothin' yet, so we will Psalm 46:10 and Exodus 14:14 this thing because we know He's going to continue to Romans 8:28 and Ephesian 3:20 our lives! Thank you for continuously supporting me and sometimes dragging me and pulling me to remain forward, focused, and following, in faith (and not fear) and favor to REmain behind the wheel of my own success! Thank you for being my confidante—a Titus in my life, as I traveled along this stretch of my glorious adventure. You constantly reminded me, that He can do all things but fail—and He's never lost a battle. Because of you, I have been able to understand and embrace the fact that sometimes we have to lose to win. I'll end this as I often do—Michelle, thank you for being my friend.

ACKNOWLEDGEMENTS

Kimberly Joy Morgan, I don't even know where to begin with my words of gratitude. You know I truly believe that everything God ordains, and I know that God used you as my real-life earth angel to help me along some of the most difficulty seasons in my life. Only He could have allowed you to reach out to me during December 2017 and allow you to encourage me as you did to "walk into the FULLNESS of who He created me to be." As you stated to me, I walked through so much in almost two years and to see me standing where I am today, I cannot thank you enough for reaching out to me so that I had the opportunity to have such an amazing and God-fearing coach supporting me along that leg of life's journey and who's still beside me now. As you continue to remind me, I did the work! Now, I pray that I am able to assist my clients in the same manner that you have helped me, and continue to help me, and many others. Thank you for sharing the JOY of our Lord and Savior with me so that I have been able to REstore the JOY that was once lost.

Lisa Moore and Montina Myers-Galloway, thank you both for the hard conversations requiring me to be vulnerable and also the conversations to truly face reality and what was evident. Your sessions allowed me to be open with my innermost feelings and learn to be comfortable and at peace with choosing me.

Paula Norwood and LaKeeva Brooks Gunderson, my ride or dies for many years. Thank you for always being with me through all of life's major events. I appreciate your listening ears and nonjudgmental support and understanding. You are true examples of real sisters, and I cherish our friendship more than words could ever explain. Looks like we need to find another pool party to attend—well at least for me!

Family-in-love: When I took my vows, I stated " . . . your family shall be my family . . . " and that is truly who you all have been, continue to be, and will always be. Paula and Bobby Don Moore, thank you for treating me as your own. Candence, Tamara, and our angel, Tia, thank you for allowing me to be your big sister. To Aunt Phil, Uncle Mike, Yoemieka "Micki," and Aunt Bea, Aunt Janet, Uncle Sonny, Miranda and Johnny "Spanky," and others, thank you for the extended family love even now.

To my other moms and dads who have assisted me along life's journey: Lugertha Morris, Bessie Froneberger, Dr. Cathy Jones, Gwen Clark, Dianne Strong-Sadler, Phyliss Caldwell, Rita Franklin, Sandra Caldwell Williams, Sara Jones, Jane Bartholomew, Denise Rasberry, Myrtle and Elton O'Neal, Valerie Belk, Brenda Norwood, Lillian and Lomax Brooks, Ellen and Willie Melton, Eunice and Jimmie

Gist, and others who I may not have listed, thank you so much for being my village and foundation.

To the special educators in my life--Linda Bost, my kindergarten teacher, Alfreda Cowan, my fifth-grade teacher, who taught me not be ashamed of being young, gifted and black. Daier Clark, my seventh-grade language arts class (which should have been classified as an honors section)—I didn't understand the symbolism of your elephants at the time, but that influenced why I wanted to be a Delta later in life. I thank you for the tough love and rigor provided to me as your student. I will never forget being moved out of your class into another class and begging my parents to allow me to return. That was the best decision that could have ever been made for I felt your passion and purpose as an educator and that is what I reflect on as an educator today. Marissa Harris, my twelfth-grade English teacher, I know I am able to speak in front of others because of the preparation I received in your class. I will forever be indebted to those of you who poured knowledge into me and allowed me to see who I could one day become.

To my sorors of Delta Sigma Theta Sorority, Incorporated, my line sisters, the Spring '97 line of the Kappa Omicron Chapter of Delta Sigma Theta Sorority, Incorporated at the University of North Carolina at Chapel Hill. A special thank you to my #8, Anitra Goodman Royster. Thank you for truly being you and showing me how to truly live life for me. To my #9, Torrey Overton Littlejohn, thank you for welcoming me and my kids into your home for my first family trip after divorce. It truly set the tone for new beginnings for me and my kids. Dr. Melita Pope Mitchell, my big sister, my colleague, my stylist, but most importantly, my friend, thank you for being my support on days where I only had enough strength to sit behind my desk. Thank you for stepping up and stepping in to lead. Thank you for the shoulder to cry on and the listening ear and thank you for imparting the importance of feeling what I need to feel, but not staying in it. Dr. Kelli Rainey, I thank you, too, for reminding me to "fix my face" during meetings to keep my personal life from impacting my professional life, but just as important, I appreciate your office being a place for me to steal away and work without having to explain my tears during the day. Dr. Anika Goodwin Hilderbrand, I have always looked up to you since my freshman year at UNC. I was always in awe of your beauty and fortitude, but I have most recently admired your strength, authenticity, and vulnerability with me via texts and conversations to encourage me during the past few years; I continue to look to you. Dr. LeTanya Love, thank you for checking me during homecoming of '17 so I would not bring harm to my reputation due to the hurt, pain, and uncertainty

ACKNOWLEDGEMENTS

I was dealing with at the time. I'm so grateful for the bond we have established in our adult lives and the late-night conversations and texts messages of encouragement. Soror cousin, Loraine Felder, thank you for being one of my first readers and continuing to encourage me, and thank you for sharing this book with your husband; that motivated me to share with a few more males to receive the male perspective on this book. Finally, to Jacqueline Wilson Coffee, Makeisha Griffin, and Marilla Montgomery, I thank God for you, and I'm so grateful that I was surrounded by your love and compassion that day in the spring of 2017 when I didn't have the strength any longer to "wear the mask" and let my guard down and cried in your presence and realized that I had to begin to choose me. Jacqueline, thank you so much for the laughter and love during my lowest times, as well as stepping in as Aunt Jackie when in need. Makeisha, thank you for sharing the book *The Seed: Finding Purpose and Happiness in Life and Work* which helped me to begin journaling and freeing my mind of so many thoughts; and Marilla, thank you for introducing me to the *3-Minute Devotional for Women (Daily Devotional),* which helped me each and every day of my year of confirmation. Jamie Adams, thank you for inviting me to worship with you that Saturday at Elevation Lake Norman. Your love, prayers, and profession as my personal legal consultant have helped me in ways that I could never repay you. To my little sister, Janelle Simmons, thank you for your gifts and talents to create the custom-made attire for our family photo.

To my first big sister, Tracey Davis Biagas. You sowed a seed on September 26, 2019 and your words of comfort, support, and encouragement assisted with me bringing this book into fruition. As you shared with me from Proverbs 18:16 (New International Version), "A gift opens the way and ushers the giver into the presence of the great." You gift has truly opened the way for me.

To Patrice McClain, the big sister I always looked up to as a little girl growing up in Friendship Missionary Baptist Church, who God ordained for me to grow closer to in my adulthood. Thank you for ALWAYS being authentically you— beautiful inside and out. You have positively impacted me in ways I could never explain, and I thank you for the many candid conversations over the past few years that helped me during some of the most challenges times of my life. I especially thank you for the referral—you were right—Lisa was no joke!

To some magnificent individuals who stretched me vocally and spiritually at Friendship Missionary Baptist Church--Dr. Tony McNeill, my first minister of music who helped me understand that everyone doesn't receive a message from a sermon. Many people rely on the music ministry, and I must be a willing vessel and use my voice to minister to others. And to Frank McInnis, thank you for the current music ministry at Friendship Missionary Baptist Church. There were many a times you asked me to prepare to sing on a Sunday. Not sure how I would hold myself together because of the things I was going through, the lyrics were just what my soul needed. To Rev. Y. Trevor Beauford and Reginald Blackmon, thank you for the messages you delivered that forever changed my life. Deacon Michael Maxwell, my photographer and my special deacon, thank you for capturing moments of transformation through confirmation in my life.

To some mighty men in my life: Antoine Calloway, you have been an amazing Godfather to my kids. Though I came to know you as a result of their father, you have truly been a brother and friend over the years as you remained neutral through confidential conversations about my life. Henry Hughie, Nathaniel Thompson, LaFarrell Little-Lloyd, thank you for giving of your time to assist me with my transition to my new home. Harold Rice, thank you for the candid conversations and male perspective as I begin again personally and maintain and grow professionally. Lamont Osborne, Patrick Griffin, Kenny Burson, and Derrick Talton, thank you for being an extension of my life as my big brothers through my birth brother.

To my siSTARS and circles in life: Shana Walker, the one who served as my unofficial counselor, my hair stylist, and thought partner—your Frankenstein loves you more than you will ever know! Shauna Graves, I get choked up each time I think about your compassion, confidentiality, grace, efficiency, and expediency with handling a major task during one of the lowest points in my life. I'm so grateful for you and Ray. Gilda Mack Benton, Kimberly Spies, Melissa Rasberry, and the Cornerstone Crew, Friends in Faith, and the ladies of Momentum Not Motion 2018, thank you for your conversations, support, and prayers. My "Cabaret Cuties" and "Flagler Crew," Victoria Flowers, Angie Green, Arlicia Parks, thank you so much for the self-care trip that allowed me to get away and feel what I needed to feel as I began a new chapter in life. To Cheryl Howard (Melvin, Chamena and Lil' Melvin), love y'all. Demetrius Wallace, my high school friend who would allow me to open up about my personal life (and kept things in confidence), who embraced me the first time I stepped foot in Elevation Church as if we had not grown distant over the years.

To my girls, "The Dance Mom's": Darnesha Eddenfield, Tiffany Webb, Kim Dow, Courtney Finney, Adrian Vollendorf. Thank you for assisting with the drop-offs, the pickups, the words of encouragement, the pictures, the hugs, and the laughs.

ACKNOWLEDGEMENTS

Lou Solomon, Linda Christopherson, and Karen Geiger, thank you for seeing something in me that I didn't even see in myself during the TWIST Conference that changed my outlook about a number of things as a leader, but most importantly as a woman.

To my colleagues in life who have been family, Dr. Zenobia Edwards, Dr. Takeem Dean, Frank Dorsey, Dr. Melvin Herring, and Dr. Jemayne King, Keisha Wilson, Tarji Caldwell, Ashley Keys, Thomas Vaughn, George Brown, and Ms. Mary, thank you for your listening ears and support. And to my leaders, Dr. Ronald L. Carter, Clarence D. Armbrister, J.D., and Dr. Karen D. Morgan, thank you for supporting me and opening up to me, sharing your personal lives as I worked through my own personal matters while striving to maintain my professionalism at work. JCSU is truly my extended family.

Though I don't personally know these individuals, I must acknowledge T.D. Jakes, Steven Furtick, Joel Osteen, Sarah Jakes Roberts, Tony Evans, Priscilla Shirer, and Pastor Keion Henderson, and many other faith leaders whose sermons and devotionals helped me through the past few years along life's journey.

Andrea Jasmin, my editor, thank you for your patience, passion, professionalism, prayers, and your craft. Your feedback, reflections, and conversations with your personal touch allowed this creation to remain my own. You truly worked to allow me to birth what was placed inside me for others to experience and hopefully be blessed by for themselves.

And finally to Y.O.U. I truly know EVERYTHING GOD ORDAINS and works for our good. Only He could have allowed you to enter my life and provide the love, support, and covering that I dreamed about and am living. You are truly an example of how He has Romans 8:28 my life. Thank you for praying for me and with me from day one without hesitation or reservations, as a God-fearing man. Thank you for being my friend and confidant as I have made some of the toughest decisions in my life. Thank you for complimenting and complementing me. I will forever be grateful for you.

PREFACE

"Create in me a clean heart, O God; and renew a right spirit within me." (Psalms 51:10 [New International Version])

RE is a prefix that means "again" or "back," and God is Jehovah Rapha—the ultimate Restorer. One thing that I have found in this life, is that our God is a God of another chance. He gives us endless opportunities to begin again, to start over— to go back and start anew. For this reason, throughout this book and through my interactions, you will see these letters capitalized which serve as continuous opportunities for me to REmain focused on the fact that I can — we all can, begin again with Him. Thus, the title of this book, *REstore the Joy: A Transformation through Confirmation.*

This book has been written to capture a time in my life where I had to literally hit my own rock bottom for me to let go and let God led me to find joy in my JOurneY, and for me to come into my own and all that He had prepared for me. I had to realize an important message written and promises in Romans 8:18-30 (NIV):

Present Suffering and Future Glory

"18I consider that our present sufferings are not worth comparing with the glory that will be revealed in us. 19For the creation waits in eager expectation for the children of God to be revealed. 20For the creation was subjected to frustration, not by its own choice, but by the will of the one who subjected it, in hope 21that the creation itself will be liberated from its bondage to decay and brought into the freedom and glory of the children of God.

22We know that the whole creation has been groaning as in the pains of childbirth right up to the present time. 23Not only so, but we ourselves, who have the first fruits of the Spirit, groan inwardly as we wait eagerly for our adoption to sonship, the redemption of our bodies. 24For in this hope we were saved. But hope that is seen is no hope at all. Who hopes for what they already have? 25But if we hope for what we do not yet have, we wait for it patiently.

26In the same way, the Spirit helps us in our weakness. We do not know what we ought to pray for, but the Spirit himself intercedes for us through wordless groans. 27And he who searches our hearts knows the mind of the Spirit, because the Spirit intercedes for God's people in accordance with the will of God.

28And we know that in all things God works for the good of those who love him, who have been called according to his purpose. 29For those God foreknew he also predestined to be conformed to the image of his Son, that he might be the firstborn among many brothers and sisters. 30And those he predestined, he also called; those he called, he also justified; those he justified, he also glorified."

I never would have imagined that I would be where I am today. I experienced four of the five most stressful events in life simultaneously: separation, moving, death of a loved one, and a medical diagnosis, but I have come to realize, with a focus on Romans 8:28, that you have to go T.H.R.O.U.G.H. (Trials, Hurt, Regrets, Obstacles, Uncertainty, Guilt, Heartbreak) to get to your BREAKTHROUGH. I once heard we cannot heal until we reveal. This is my Exodus and may it be a REvelation for you.

ENJOY!

There is no greater agony than bearing an untold story inside you.
~ Maya Angelou

CHAPTER 1

Crazy In Love

It was a weekend in June after my recent graduation from college. I and my closest childhood friends were headed to a pool party thrown by my brother and some of his coworkers. With no cares in the world, but whatever we had to look forward to in this thing called adult life, we were excited about the opportunity to just share in an evening of fun as we had many times before in junior high and high school. As we approached the event while singing, laughing, and reminiscing, I blurted out, "We're going to find our husbands tonight!" Even now I giggle at my statement, not realizing the true power of the words we speak. I can hear one of my friend's responses right now as clearly as I did in that moment. LaKeeva said, "Girl! You are crazy!" We all burst out in laughter, not realizing what was actually about to happen to impact many years of my life. That night, I in fact, met my husband.

This wasn't our first encounter. I actually recall "officially" meeting him for the very first time during my spring break of my senior year at the University of North Carolina at Chapel Hill. I returned home to Charlotte for the break and my brother invited me to come join him and some of his friends from work for lunch. So, I reached out to my friend, LaKeeva, who was also home from North Carolina A&T State University and asked her to join me. We arrived at the restaurant with my brother and his friends already seated. When we approached the table, all eyes were on us. My brother greeted me and introduced us to everyone, and as we were taking the empty seats at the table, this guy says, "What are y'all freshmen?!"

Feeling somewhat insulted, because I was in fact finished with my degree at this point, but awaiting commencement, I responded with a major attitude, "Baby we are graduating seniors!" As he laughed, I thought to myself, Who is this immature guy?! I would never give a guy like him the time of day. Well, I learned to never say never.

When I returned home after graduation, my family threw me a graduation cookout. My closest friends and family were in attendance, and as usual, my brother invited some of his people, as many had become just like family. Unbeknownst to me, he and my future husband had become closer as my brother served as his direct supervisor. Unfamiliar with his car, I walked out into the front yard to see who had arrived, and to my surprise, "Mr. Immature" along with his then girlfriend exited from the car. Being that I am the kind of person that I am, I was cordial as he wished me congratulations and proceeded to join everyone else in the backyard. I rejoined my friends in the backyard but made it a point to act as if he wasn't even in attendance; I definitely didn't extend an invitation. Quite honestly, I cannot remember anything else at this point but the fact that fate (I thought at the time) would lead us back to each other in only a few days at a pool party.

When my girls and I arrived at the party, we immediately headed toward the pool, but didn't get in because we had recently gotten tattoos and were avoiding the water. We sat around the pool area, laughing and joking with the people we knew. After a while, we decided to enter the clubhouse area where DJ Tut was set up on the ones and twos. There were so many familiar faces in the place, including, my ex-boyfriend, whom I had been in a relationship with on and off since junior high school. He had broken my heart the summer after my sophomore year in college, and at that point in life, I had decided that I wouldn't be in another relationship until after I graduated from college. Don't get me wrong, I had a few friends and flings here and there, but nothing that would keep me from focusing on finishing my degree without distractions.

When I saw my ex, he approached me and we embraced, but I was in no way interested in rekindling anything, and I made sure to show him rather than tell him, for actions speak louder than words. As we hugged, my eyes immediately focused in on my future husband. Working to use anything to get away from my ex, I bee lined towards him and just started dancing and making small talk. I thought this would be a good distraction, because this man knew I didn't even have the smallest bit of interest in him, so this would be the best decoy. As I danced close to him, we began to engage in conversation, and in an attempt to ignore our initial encounter, I let my guard down and began to go with the flow.

The encounter at the pool party led to phone conversations, and phone conversations led to dates. He seemed to be so different from the guys I had dated before. I can remember my first interaction with him and one of his little sisters. He was so protective but gentle; I felt if he treated her like that, he would definitely do the same for me. I was further drawn to him because of the fact that he was quiet and very much reserved, was employed, and didn't have any children. I love children, but I didn't want to have to deal with any baby momma drama as I began to establish an intimate relationship with this man. To my surprise, we really clicked. We spent hours and hours talking about our dreams and aspirations, music, and just laughing at things in life. I fell in love with the little things he would do for me, like helping me decorate my first classroom as a seventh-grade teacher, to making me CDs with songs that I loved and sneaking and leaving them in my car. This guy seemed to be nothing like any others I had met before. Was this because he was a few years older than me or was he truly just different? I wasn't sure at the time, but I fell madly in love, and there was literally nothing I would not do for him.

A few months into our relationship, we planned to go with his family to the beach for Labor Day. This would actually be my first trip with him, and I was more than excited. As we prepared for the trip, his little sister was upset because she wanted to go but had to march with her high school band that Friday night and the family planned to leave at that time. So, I volunteered the both of us to go to the game and watch her march, and then get on the road afterwards.

That Friday night the three of us left for the beach, and while we were en route we began to approach a police checkpoint. He was driving at the time, I was asleep in the passenger seat, and his sister was knocked out in the back. I was awakened by him in somewhat of a panic. As I felt him take his foot off the accelerator in his Mitsubishi Diamante, he exclaimed, "Hey, switch seats with me!" Somewhat out of it and confused, I said, "Huh?!" He responded again, but with a look of concern, "Hurry up! Switch seats with me!" Not really coherent after being awakened from my sleep and being naïve, I unbuckled my seatbelt and somehow, we both managed to switch sides while the car was still in motion, crossing over the gear and console, repositioning ourselves and buckling up before rolling to a stop at the checkpoint.

McBee is an area in South Carolina that is already known as a speed trap and definitely a place where we didn't want to get in any trouble with the law. "License and registration," the officer asked as he shined a flashlight into the car. I grabbed my purse from the backseat and opened the console to retrieve the car registration. Once cleared to proceed on our route, I pulled into the parking lot of the nearest gas station confused and wanting to know what just happened. Peering over the backseat, seeing his sister still sound asleep, he stated, "I don't have a license." Young and immature, I was like, "Ok."

Ok? Really, Laura! You just risked your life and reputation. This was only the first of many signs that I should have listened to my gut, but I was young, and crazy in love.

In 2002, I had informed him that I didn't know how long I could take us being in a long-distance relationship. His job relocated him to Chicago for some time, and I spent my holidays and long weekends traveling back and forth to be with him. To my surprise, not long after I made this comment, he informed me that the contract associated with the company he worked for was being terminated in Chicago and he would be returning home. Not too long after his return, he would propose to me.

I remember the day clearly. At that time, I had moved in with him, but had actually begun the process for buying my first home. I had been pre-approved and was working to decide which side of Charlotte I wanted to reside. Since he was back and we did everything together, we would take drives in the evenings to check out both new and established neighborhoods. This particular afternoon after work, we had plans to go out to dinner. As I was getting myself ready, he kept going in and out of the apartment and seemed somewhat disheveled. When I approached the car to get in, he got out of the driver's seat and went to the trunk of the car. After rambling around and patting his jacket, he entered the car and drove off.

We arrived at an Italian restaurant that we enjoyed on the east side called Mama Lena's. As we sat at the table awaiting our food, we each began to make a list on our napkins of the things we wanted in a home. We shared with one another and had more similarities than differences. After dinner, he drove towards downtown to the spot where we always sat outside and enjoyed people watching. It was somewhat chilly that evening in March and my attitude showed that I was not feeling sitting outside. For the first time that I could recall he became frustrated with me, but he decided to change plans and suggested that we ride around and look at housing developments. We rode around for about an hour and then decided we would go and check in on his family. As we turned onto the highway, I felt tension and saw it on his face as well. I asked, "What's wrong with you?" He looked at me and said, "I was trying to do something, but here." And he threw a small red gift box in my lap. I was speechless and shocked, but I didn't want to make any assumptions of what was inside—I mean it could be a pair of earrings. I opened the box, and as I expected and was hoping, there was a ring. I looked at him and he said, "I've been trying to find the right time to give this to you, but you didn't want to sit outside at our favorite spot." My dream was about to come true; I was going to get married! I hugged him, kissed him, and then proceeded to call my parents. After I got off the phone with them, my now fiancé began to tell me how he went to my parents' home and asked my dad for my hand in marriage, but my dad responded, "No!" and walked away from him. It's sometimes hard to tell if my dad is serious or joking, but a few seconds later, he returned and said, "She's expensive! Are you going to be able to handle that and take care of her, because she can always come home?" He assured him that he could and would, and said my dad eventually said yes.

In less than a year, the morning had arrived for me to walk down the aisle. That morning I awoke very early to meet my hairstylist at her salon. When I arrived, there sat my dad's truck in front of her shop. I wondered why in the world he was there, but as usual, he knew what time I would be there and wanted to pay for it. He seemed rather sad and as if he wanted to say something but never did. I guess this was somewhat of a loss for him, and he was working to enjoy the final moments before he would give me away.

The time had finally arrived as some of the last guests were allowed to be seated in the balcony and my father and I would begin the journey down one of the long aisles in my home church. What I had waited a lifetime for was actually taking place, and only a few minutes later, I was now someone's wife. In my mind, I was now free from my parents (specifically my father) and able to stand—not even alone—but alongside this individual who vowed with me to make God the center of our lives and be as one, and verbally committing, "Entreat me not to leave the, or to return from following after thee . . ." (Ruth 1:16 [King James Version]).

CHAPTER 2

Life & Favor

T he morning of February 3rd, 2018, God revealed that there was a book in me. As I laid in bed, I had begun my daily ritual of prayer, and then I would rise to read my daily devotionals in *Daily Readings: The Power of I Am,* by Joel Osteen; *3-Minute Devotions for Women* by Barbour Publishing and Rick Warren's *The Purpose Driven Life*. This particular morning, my phone contained GroupMe notifications from both my prayer group as well as my line sister group. Normally, I would look at the messages in my prayer group before any others, because they would support my morning time alone with God, but on this particular Saturday morning I was led to see what my sorority sisters were discussing. One of my nineteen amazing line sisters (the women that would go through an initiation process with me in college to join a Black Greek Letter organization) was telling the group about how she had been asked to talk to the youth of her home church during Black History Month. She couldn't understand why she had been chosen, and talked about how she could not tell the woman whom she had known her whole life, no. She said, "but who would want to hear me talk in church?!" This made me reflect on what I learned by attending the ACE Spectrum Executive Leadership Program (Cohort 3) in April 2014.

We all have a story to share.

"If someone can see something in you, then you should definitely open up your
eyes and see that something in yourself." ˜~ Dr. Laura Colson

God has moved me to tell my story, and he gave me the courage to do so on that same Saturday morning. As I was listening to my Pandora station, a song that I always loved and that always did "something" to me inside each time I heard it came on, and it was confirmation. I always knew the chorus of the song, but I never honestly paid attention to the title until this particular morning: "Life and Favor." This song, written by Pastor John P. Kee, helps frame this journey of my life and testimony you are about to experience in this book. The song basically relays the message that sometimes we don't look like what we have been through in life; and that is my testimony.

I know there are people who have looked at my life and thought that I have it all together, and I have the things that many hope, wish, and dream about, but they don't know my story. Because of being a native Charlottean and still residing in the area, and due to social media, my community has pretty much been able to follow me along the years. From attending the University of North Carolina at Chapel Hill, to beginning my teaching career in the Charlotte-Mecklenburg School System, to marriage, then transitioning into higher education, the birth of my children, to business owner, to doctor, and dean. From that lens, things look aligned, unaltered—the ideal dreams, goals, aspirations accomplished, but this is far from the case.

I worked to live my best life, so I thought, but I did what was expected of me by others. For the most part, I was the ideal child, had not gotten in a lot of trouble growing up. I did well academically and socially, and in many aspects, I followed in the footsteps of my older brother. I married and then had children. I became a business owner and advanced up the ranks in my field. But that is what it was like from the outside looking in.

Sadly, I lived a life for others and not for myself. As a result, I suffered on the inside from pain and depression, and I lost my faith. As much as others believed in me, I didn't believe in myself. I lived with a lot of regret, but my life forever changed in 2017. My life began to transform as God truly showed me how He works everything for our good.

I hope you enjoy and benefit from how speaking my truth has allowed God to restore the joy.

CHAPTER 3

Twist Conference

O ne day I decided to pick up a book that I received from a conference that I attended when I was promoted at work in 2014. When I picked up the book a CD fell out, and I immediately thought about what was on it. That spring I was selected by my University's Executive Vice President to attend a conference with a close colleague and friend. The TWIST Conference for Women was started in 2011 by Lou Solomon (whom I would meet) and Carson Tate. They were tired of the same old boring women's conferences with too many people, no intimacy, and not getting to the deep issues. In that frustration they created the TWIST Conference for Women in Leadership with a goal to be a *twist* on a traditional conference for women. It would be intimate, for only 40 women or less, where women could bond and talk about real issues.

One activity that took place on the first full day was to be videotaped in front of this group of women who I did not know and speak on the cusp about an experience. I recall one of the speakers of the conferences talking to me during a break and asking me if I do public speaking, and I quickly responded, "NO!" She said that I should consider doing so. I never watched the recording to see what she saw until this day three years later. As I loaded the disc, I saw myself and this is the transcription of what I said to the group.

"I'm Laura, and good morning to you all. If you look around this room right now, this was my life, all the way up until junior high school. I asked, 'Does anybody

see what this room is composed of?' The group responded almost in unison, 'Mostly white (women).' So, my parents—wonderful parents, and educators. Growing up I never knew what struggle was. They did the best for me. Where we lived, I was sheltered because my parents never let me stay home by myself. They wanted me to see what I could see within the city limits, but like I said growing up, this was like my classroom. I was one of the few African Americans and for the most part, I would be the only female African American in many of my 'academically gifted' classes. During that time kids like myself would be pulled out from their regular classes to interact with another teacher and students because of our 'higher level thinking.' But I have come to deal with that, and I hate to say deal with it—I've come to grow from it. I think some of my best friends in life are not African American.

As of recently though, I really think I started growing. I'm a native Charlottean—grew up right here. I have an older brother, who is seven years older than I am. In high school I was top of my class, just like others of you in here, but my turning point in life was when my guidance counselor said to me, 'You want to go to Chapel Hill?! Why don't you go to an HBCU (Historically Black Colleges and Universities)?' As tears formed in my eyes I spoke, 'That hurt.' Because I was like, I'm like everyone else here, I'm a scholar athlete, you know, I'm well rounded, I do community service. Who is she to tell me I should go to an HBCU? Now granted, I received a scholarship to attend an HBCU, but I turned it down just because of that. That was a challenge for me, and I took that challenge head on.

I went to Chapel Hill, but I wasn't as successful as I had been in the past. I went off to school and was free; dealt with depression; struggled freshman year. But something inside me woke up and said: 'Remember what your guidance counselor said to you—you can't fail.' And so, I have been driving myself ever since.

Moving forward, since I started working at Johnson C. Smith University (JCSU), I've just started living my life. I've encountered many challenges that I would not speak about before, but you all have made this conference very personable for me and an opportunity for me to grow and release myself."

Watching that recording began to bring back a lot of memories for me, but it also began to put some things in perspective about my life at the time. As I was told by my husband, I was responsible for my own happiness, and in that moment, I realized that I was truly miserable.

CHAPTER 4

Entreat Me

I was overwhelmed and frustrated with things in life. Though my husband and I were working full-time jobs and managing businesses on the side, we still struggled with paying bills. Life was filled with work and neglecting myself to ensure the needs of others were met. We could never see eye to eye on how to manage money. I felt like I was the one who wanted to budget and save, whereas he seemed to be the one who wanted to live for the day. This is not what I was expecting at this time in my life, particularly when it came to marriage.

I recall in 2003 when we attended premarital counseling, we were advised that three things are major in marriage: communication, sex, and finances. After being married for five years, all three of these matters were taking a toll on our relationship; communication seemed to be the root of all evil. Reflecting back over the years, communication had always been a concern of mine. Not soon after our wedding, our intimate conversations dwindled. The newness of our relationship was gone, and we were getting into a routine. My husband had never been a man of many words, and I always told him I felt like he had a wall built up that prevented me from completely entering into his emotional life. Now, I know that most men aren't in touch, or as open with their emotional side, but in my gut, there was something different about this wall that would eventually be broken down in 2017.

I believe I was very vulnerable with my conversations, feelings, goals, and aspirations at the beginning of our relationship and marriage; however, as time passed and life changed, I found myself internalizing everything. This was not what I thought marriage was going to be like from my experience growing up. T.D. Jakes's "Men Play Games Very Well" (2017) comes to mind as I try to explain this. In this particular sermon by Jakes, he says:

> "Women have been trained for relationships all of their lives. Remember when you got your first Barbie and Ken . . . and you were playing house with them. You have been practicing since you were five years old for the big day, and that is why you become so disappointed . . . you have a degree in relationships. We do not train our boys in relational skills . . . While you were learning relationships, we were learning to play games, and the thing that men do very, very well is play games . . . men play games because games have rules—they have potential of winning and you score points. And anything that has rules and scoring and winning, men do well . . . and that is why with dating men call it scoring, because he thought relationships were a game, because men play games well. That's why men go to work and make money...because it's just how we keep score . . . but the only problem is when somebody changes the rules of the game and the man can't score points, he gets frustrated and starts losing. And when a man starts losing, he starts dying because he can't figure out what went wrong, because he can't score points and he's not winning . . . and his self-esteem comes down. And anytime a man can't figure out how to win a game he becomes angry, bitter, and confused."

It makes sense now. My husband was out of the "game." He was no longer able to keep score, so he turned to his work for scoring. I always talked to him about how our relationship was changed because of his lawn and landscape business. As much as I tried to support it, I hated it. Now that I think about it—its place in his life felt like another woman. I unknowingly became jealous of it. All of his attention was focused on it. From sunup to sundown, he was with it. He became too tired as a result of it and no longer wanted to talk to me after work. I began to feel like I didn't matter; I was no longer the center of his attention and I began to retreat. My retreating consisted of me shifting my focus and all of my attention to my career and no longer pouring out my thoughts and feelings to him—as I was losing my joy.

Our lives both became occupied day and night with our careers—him leaving early in the mornings to begin his schedule as a landscaper, working well into the evening, not returning home until after the sun had gone down. I was just as occupied, teaching during the day, and attending classes in the evening. Most time during the weeknights were spent eating dinner and attempting to discuss our day or watching television together. The date nights began to dwindle because one or both of us was either tired or we just didn't feel up to crowds and deciding what to do or where to go. I began to feel like we were drifting apart and suggested that we should consider going to counseling. I mean during our premarital counseling we were told that counseling was available for couples to use throughout their marriage. What I thought was a good idea wasn't received well and was pretty much blown off. So, I decided to just do some reading on my own as to what I could do as a wife. As I would read books, I would work to share information and wanted my husband to take part in some of the reading and activities that I found interesting. Some things he was cool about and others, not so much. I wondered sometimes if it was just a phase and maybe I was worrying too much.

Life began to seem more like routine. We would rise in the morning, sometimes he would leave out before me and other days I wasn't sure when his day would begin. When I returned in the evenings there was rarely a day when he wasn't home before me, unless there was inclement weather. It got to a point that we were barely talking. When I married him, I knew he was a man of few words. When I first met his stepdad he said, "I can't believe you got him to talk to you!" as he smiled and laughed and embraced me. But I was beginning to feel like I was a bother when I tried to find out how his day had gone. Most of the time he would come in and just sit, seeming to not want to be disturbed. Even if dinner was ready, he wouldn't eat until later. In my soul I felt like something wasn't right. I would always ask if everything was ok, and receive the normal response, "Yeah." Maybe it was stress from being an entrepreneur that I didn't understand. I was unsure and it was making me a bit self-conscious as to whether or not I was supporting him as I should as his wife.

Since leaving the school system and starting a position at Johnson C. Smith University, I began coming home and telling him of the things that were occurring for me in my new role. I wanted to share things with him, but I also wanted to hear about his business and how things were going. He told me things were good and he had a crew working for him. This was exciting news to me and I asked if there was anything I could do to help and what he foresaw in his business plan. Most of the time he asked me to assist with invoicing and developing advertisements to distribute. Other than that, I never really knew what went on with the business. I do know that he was taking care of what he was financially responsible for, from what I could tell.

Then one day I came home, and the garage door wouldn't open, which caught me off guard. Maybe it was the battery in the remote that needed to be replaced. So, I entered the house through the front door. As I entered, I flipped the switch to the light, and it didn't turn on. Maybe there was a power outage. When I went back outside to check the mail, I noticed the television on through my neighbor's window. I took my cell phone out of my pocket and called my best friend, Paula, who actually worked for the power company. I said, "Hey. My power is off, and I don't know why." She said, "Let me check something." She put me on hold for a minute, and when she returned, she said, "Girl, your bill hasn't been paid in a few months." Embarrassed and in disbelief, I responded, "Huh?" I'm sure he paid the bill. She said, "Nope, but this is what I'm going to do. I'm going to turn it back on, but you have got to get it caught up in the next day or two." I said, "Of course. Thank you, and I'll call you back when I figure out what's going on."

That evening when my husband came home, I told him we needed to talk. I informed him that when I got home the power was off and I had to contact Paula to get it turned on. I asked, "Why haven't you paid the bill?" He responded, "I forgot." I said, "She told me they don't cut the power off unless you are months behind." He said, "I guess I just lost track of things. I'll get it paid." I responded, "When?" "I'll get it done." He replied. I said, "Well I can do it if you need me to." He assured me that he had it, so I trusted him. At this point he had not really given me a reason not to.

Since business was growing for him, I sought an opportunity to keep myself busy, but also work towards my career goals and enrolled in a doctoral program. At this time, we didn't have any kids, and I felt that this time would be the best for me to go back to school again to assist with creating new opportunities and hopefully another promotion in my profession. Most people know that in order to make money as an educator you must work towards a terminal degree. I began looking for programs at colleges and universities in the area and began to study for the GRE exam. I normally studied at night in the bedroom while he would watch television downstairs. One night when he came upstairs to shower before bed, I was working as usual and his cell phone rang. Trying to focus, I reached over to silence it. Before I could get situated again on my side of the bed a text came through, and I looked at it and it read, "I miss you." My body filled with heat and my heart rate went up. Who was texting him saying they missed him this late at night? When he came out of the shower, he looked at me and could tell something was wrong. I said, "Who is she?!" He said, "Who is what, Laura?!" "Look at your phone! She said she misses you!" Bee lining to his side of the bed, he grabbed his phone off of the nightstand and said, "That's my customer! She must mean she missed me cutting her grass."

I wasn't buying that excuse, even if she was a customer. "Well why does it say she misses you?" All he could say was, "I don't know." I said, "Call her!" He responded, "I'm not calling her!" I said, "She just called. Call her back!" He refused. He tried to assure me that it wasn't what I thought. I began to ask if this is why he comes home at all hours of the night. Was she why even on rainy days he wasn't home? He remained adamant that it wasn't what I thought, but my heart didn't believe it. I told him, "You need to get rid of her as a customer! And you need to make sure you are doing everything in your power to let me know that I am the only one in your life." Maybe I had jumped to conclusions. Was I overreacting? Things were never really the same for me after that night.

After a few days of functioning in silence, we somehow began to speak again. I asked him if he would go to counseling with me. As before, he didn't understand the point of it, but I just asked him to go for me if nothing else. He agreed. We went to one session. I felt like we should go again, but I didn't even feel like asking. Even when I asked before, he wouldn't go willingly, and this time I only felt he went because of the text message from his customer. I realized that if I was responsible for anything, it was myself. So, I worked to read books and even went to counseling by myself. The only person that I could do anything about would be me. I had taken vows with him and before God, and I believed that only death do us part.

Feeling emotionally neglected, I worked to cover up what I was feeling by pouring into work. After leaving the school system and beginning my career in higher education, I began working on my doctorate. Halfway through my doctoral program I found out that I was expecting our first child. In my eyes our relationship had not been the best, but definitely wasn't the worst. Maybe this child would refocus us on one another. Our firstborn was definitely a blessing, but the process and responsibilities that came with parenting would only cause me to question whether or not this marriage thing was for me as we seemed to grow further and further apart.

I recall leaving my job on a Friday afternoon and driving a little over an hour to Gardner-Webb University where I would begin my first doctoral course. I would spend the evenings from six o'clock until sometimes ten o'clock in class with a cohort of other working adults over the next two years of my life. I would turn around and drive back home, only to return to the campus by nine o'clock the next morning for a class that would not end until five o'clock in the evening. That first day of class some of our instructors met with us to discuss what we were embarking upon as doctoral students. They discussed a lot of things, but the one thing that still sticks out in my memory to this day is the fact that one instructor stated some of us would end up divorced. That really caught me by surprise. Why in the world would obtaining a degree result in separation? Hindsight is always twenty-twenty, and I had to fight my damnedest not to become a statistic.

I enrolled in the doctoral program not only to accomplish my goals of reaching the highest educational efficiency possible, but also for my family. I have always wanted to provide for my family the way that my parents did for me and my brother. Advancing in my career by obtaining my degree was the only way for me to increase my salary in the education field. I was striving to ensure my children would have a better life than I did. Unfortunately, it did not seem to me that my husband was as supportive of this decision as I thought he was initially. When he started coming home at the end of the week, only for me to be headed to class, I sensed he didn't like it. He was short with me and became more and more distant. There were many trips to and from work where I spent the entire time crying and wondering what was going to happen to our relationship. At one point when I was heading home late on Friday nights after class, and calling to let him know I was en route, he would respond that he was out with his friends. At first, I didn't have a problem with it, but eventually this began to take its toll on my trust. I was already on an emotional roller coaster working full-time and enrolled as a student, and to add more fuel to the fire, I suffered from the sickness and emotional ups and downs that come with pregnancy.

My mind and gut felt like my husband was cheating on me, but I could not prove it, nor did I want to because the thought of it brought more instability with my emotional state as a pregnant woman. Now this was not the first time in my marriage when I felt there may have been infidelity, or should I say this was the second time there were signs of unfaithfulness. There was evidence that I ignored not even two years into our marriage. But being the strong woman that I am, I denied my feelings and continued on. I never opened up to my husband about how I was feeling. I didn't want to seem like I didn't trust him. Anytime I did express a concern, he would always say, "You're never here, so I just go out with my boys."

My response was always, "I'm doing this for us." We never really argued but seemed to work to avoid confrontation altogether. I never really voiced my true feelings to the one that I should have been able to discuss anything with, and then one afternoon, it happened.

I came home from work and was about to continue the work on my dissertation proposal on our home computer. I logged in and his email was open. My heart began to pound, and I could feel the throbbing in my head. I became hot all over and began to feel uneasy. I would not deny myself this time. Yes, I looked through the emails to see if all this time my gut had been right. I was almost faint and could feel the pounding of my heart throbbing in my head. I had become heated from the adrenaline rush and hormones of pregnancy. Right before my very eyes was a communication chain between him and another woman, speaking about each other and what they were interested in doing with each other. As much as I wanted to see if there were other communications, this one was more than enough.

I lashed out in anger, hurt, and frustration: "What the hell is this?!" "Who is this, a customer?" He tried to console me as he attempted to explain to me that the conversation didn't mean anything, but you couldn't tell me otherwise. He said, "It's not what you think!" "What do you mean it's not what I think?! It is written plain as day!" I yelled. "Nothing happened, for real," he pleaded. "You expect me to believe that?" I questioned. By this time, I am at the point of hyperventilation, and bent over with a sharp pain. I threatened, "If I lose this baby because of this I WILL NEVER FORGIVE YOU!" Inconsolable, he tried to calm me and further explain. "I have felt lonely, and I needed someone to talk to." Devastated, I give him the evil eye. "Lonely? Needed someone to talk to? You never talk to me! Every day I try to talk to you to find out how things are with the business, what is going on with your life, and you act as if I am bothering you. So instead of badgering you, I leave you alone. So, you turn to someone else?! These conversations have nothing to do with loneliness!" Balled up on the couch devastated—I completely lost my joy.

What was I to do? I was eight months pregnant, I thought that everyone perceived us as having the ideal marriage. I took my vows for better or for worse. Had he really cheated or was he just engaged in conversations? Regardless, there was an emotional attachment of some sort I believed. What did I do to deserve this?! I lost all trust in my husband, but I did what I thought I was supposed to do instead of what my soul felt. I wanted to leave, but I didn't know how. What would people think? I didn't want my child to grow up without a mother and father in the home.

I didn't want my marriage to fail. So, I ignored my feelings and stayed. I was completely broken inside and had a feeling of betrayal. I was angry and unable to forgive or forget. He promised me that he had not cheated on me, and that he would do whatever it took to make things better. Again, this wasn't the first time he made this promise and failed to keep it. In full denial of what my intuition was telling me and what my eyes had seen, I told him that he would have to treat me like a queen and make me feel like I was the only woman for him. This he promised, but things would never be the same for us in my heart and my mind.

I could not love him the way I once did. The examples of marriage that I witnessed over the years consisted of men and women being married for years. I saw no evidence of "the worse" in marriages. When I took my vows, they were between us and God and were not meant to be broken. I was stuck and stuck in misery at this point in my life. I had to fight internally to fall in love with him again, but I felt I had to wear the mask so that we could continue to "look" like the perfect married couple in society's eyes. I was so worried about what other people thought. Then God blessed us with our firstborn.

In 2008, our son came along and provided me a way to pour my love into him. He was the best thing that could have happened to me at that time. He became my focus, my drive, my everything—my why.

Continuing to play the role of the ideal wife, though scorned, I felt that since I was on maternity leave, I would bear the brunt of responsibilities associated with a colicky newborn. I didn't realize how difficult it was to care for such a small bundle, and I became overwhelmed and suffered from postpartum depression. But with everything else that I had endured, I internalized everything, and didn't express to my husband my true feelings. There would be many a nights and days that all I did was cry. I didn't know how to ask for help and I really didn't want any help. I had suffered so long internally, I didn't know how to cry out for help, and I just learned how to deal for years to come.

For about seven years we began to grow apart, in my eyes. He was focused on his business, and I was focused on advancing in my career. From time to time, we would catch ourselves and attempt to make time for one another. I realized I took my vows between us and God, which said for better or for worse—I felt stuck. From what I grew to understand growing up in the church and within a two-parent home, divorce was not an option. He wasn't doing anything to bring me harm physically. I knew I loved him, but I was questioning his love for me. And since I didn't believe in divorce, I felt my only option was to just pray and deal with it.

CHAPTER 5

Second Time Around

Transitions and opportunities in life continued to unfold for me from pouring into work and hiding from life, but I found myself hesitating more and more about whether or not I should seek opportunities for advancement. I always wanted more in life, but my husband seemed to come off as content with where he was and where we were collectively. In my eyes I was the breadwinner, but I didn't want to be. I desired what I had seen and read about the man being the head of household and covering the wife. Though things were paid, finances were tight, but I don't think he truly realized it, because I always seemed to make things happen. I think he assumed I had more money than I let it be known, but in actuality, I knew the importance of "taking care of home" and "pinching a penny" when necessary and avoiding "robbing Peter to pay Paul". That's what I learned growing up.

I can recall my childhood, from a toddler being raised up in an apartment with my parents, my brother, and for a period of time, my grandmother on my dad's side. I also remember my parents working multiple jobs to purchase a home that we moved into the summer before sixth grade. My parents always provided for me and my older brother--they never allowed us to experience struggle; well, at least they hid it well in front of us. We were not rich, but my parents always seemed to make a way to not only provide the necessities in life, but also many of the things that I wanted. However, as an adult, I began to wonder whether or not this was a good thing.

In 2010 the opportunity came for me to be promoted from an assistant director position to director, but I hesitated to discuss it with my husband because he never really seemed happy for me when I discussed opportunities for promotion or acknowledgements of the work I was doing. I felt like he resented me or as if I thought I was better than him. So, with this position, I worked to downplay it, as if it was not a big deal for me, but just a way to make more money. Luckily, it came at the perfect time, because shortly thereafter, we would be expecting our second child, and to my surprise the downfall of my husband's business.

I can recall the evening that I found out that my husband's business plummeted. I came home from my usual hectic day at work, and he was sitting in the dining room. I knew something was up because this was a room that we rarely used outside of holidays. So, I began the normal evening exchange between husband and wife, inquiring as to how his day had gone. Always a man of few words, he said it was ok, but his eyes showed otherwise, and my instinct felt something else. I asked what was wrong, and he sat there for a minute. Knowing that there was something he needed to get off his chest, I interrogated him: "What is it? Are you sick? Did something happen at work?" In this short amount of time, I became aggravated because I shouldn't have had to work this hard to get an answer from my husband who is supposed to be able to talk to me about anything. Then it happened. "I lost some contracts," he responded. I know my eyes probably showed my shock, but if he only knew what was going on inside. I responded as a "supportive wife" should, "It's going to be ok."

IT'S GOING TO BE OK?! Who was I fooling?! Inside I was on fire! In a few seconds I replayed all the conversations we have had since he decided to quit his full-time job and start his own business. The ones where I kept saying we must ensure he paid himself by putting money away in savings. I'd ask, "What is the backup plan if you get injured because of the physical requirements of the job?" To be honest, I never felt the business was a good idea in the first place, but again, as a "supportive wife" I wanted him to follow his dream. I thought to myself, *I knew this shit was going to happen*! I was filled with mixed emotions. I reached out to embrace him, letting him know that I was empathetic, but thinking to myself *I am pissed*. At this point, there was no need to fuss about it, because what was done was done; however, I am Ms. Control Freak, and I began to panic as to how we are going to pay bills with one income.

He was unemployed for a few months, and this was one of the most hellish times of my life—I was losing my joy. I had a lot of resentment and all that went through my head during this time was, *If he would have just listened to me.* I didn't know how to deal with the situation, so I just focused on work—that was my escape, but more importantly, I felt I had to go above and beyond. I didn't want to risk the thought of losing my job. Each day I would come home from work, worn out from the day, and pick up my son from my mother who kept him, cook dinner or pick up something, and come home to a man who was just existing. Most days I would come home, and he would be in the same spot—in the family room on the couch. There was very little conversation between us, because I didn't want to nag him, but I did want to know what he was doing about finding a job. At first, I would just check on him, and then work on my classwork as I was working to finish my doctorate. This got old real quick, especially when it came time to pay bills. After the first few weeks, I began to get frustrated at the fact that I would come home, and nothing had been done in the house. He was there all day, and it seemed that he didn't lift a finger. I didn't fuss, but just sucked it up and did what I had always done, since according to society, "the house is a reflection of the woman." So finally, one day I asked if he had any job leads. He responded, "I'm working to try to get some bids out for some new contracts." I said, "But what about something temporary?" "Nah, I gotta rebuild my business." I thought to myself, *WHAT*?! Contracts aren't awarded overnight, and we have bills to pay! I thought he was just being stubborn and refusing to accept the fact that his business may be over. So, I took it upon myself to start searching for jobs for him. He had been self-employed for six years and didn't have a resume that reflected his entrepreneurial skills, so I created one for him. I spent the time in the evening that I was not working on my classwork completing job applications for him online and inquiring with my network for any leads. I began to wonder why I was putting more effort into generating an income for him than he was! However, being in the "Ms. Fix It" mode, I failed to realize that my husband might have been suffering from depression.

After a long day at work, I came home to our usual routine, but on this particular day I just flat out asked him, "Do you not want to work?" For the past few months, I was "robbing Peter to pay Paul." We didn't really have savings, and what little bit I had we depleted in no time. I would alternate paying certain bills every other month. I'd take advantage of my parents and their offers to take us out to dinner and "shop" in their pantry; saying to them, "I just need a few things and don't want to stop at the grocery store." I took advantage of my refund checks from school and got the maximum return I could in order to assist with paying our bills. At the very end of the month when things were extremely tight, I would cash in money from my change jar, just to make it to payday. I felt so lonely. I didn't want people to know what was going on in my life, and pride was the main factor. I cared deeply for my husband, and I felt that if I talked to people about this matter, regardless of how close to us they were, as a man his pride would be hurt. I internalized everything that I was feeling and experiencing—and was dying inside. I was overwhelmed, depressed, scared, frustrated, but mostly, I was angry. Why did it seem that I was more worried about him than he was for himself? Thankfully, reality was finally revealed, and because of this life changing event, my husband would finally begin a new career.

After I questioned him about not wanting to work, he finally opened up to me and I realized that he truly may have been suffering from depression. He had never been unemployed in his life. This was the first time since he started working as a teenager that he wasn't generating any income. This really hit me, and I could completely understand; I have been working since I was fourteen. So, I asked him what he wanted to do, and he remained adamant about rebuilding his business. Instead of me getting mad about that, I worked to respect his determination, but I was not about to let him sit in the house and not contribute in some manner while I worked tirelessly each day. So, I asked him about the leads that he was receiving as a result of the applications that I had completed for him. He had some reservations because he didn't want to return to working for someone else. As he held our son during our conversation, something triggered a thought in my head. "You should try substitute teaching," I said to him. At this time in his life when he had gotten used to telling other people what to do, he could definitely tell kids what to do. Also, substitute teaching would allow him to decide if and when he wanted to work (even though I felt he needed to work every day and as much as he could). There was some hesitation about this suggestion from me, but I encouraged him to just try it. He definitely had options because we lived in one of the largest school systems in the country, and he could pick from working with elementary, middle, or high school students; most importantly, this would generate some income and get him out of the house.

As a result of this idea, my husband was able to find work. After experiencing working with different age groups, he found his niche at the high school level, and in his area of expertise—drafting. I thanked God that he was able to not only find employment but find a career that would allow him to use his degree, touch the lives of our future, and for his sake— allow him to rebuild his business on the side. He was coming out of what seemed to be a depressive state and decided to take the necessary steps to become a licensed teacher, and I worked to support him, but things weren't as good as I thought they would be. When he enrolled in his lateral entry courses, I felt as if he was expecting me to do his work. All three of my degrees were in education, but I was not about to do the work for him to get credit. The same way I had to work full-time and complete coursework; he was going to have to endure the same. Reflecting on it now, I must have made doing this look simple over the years, because I could sense his anger and frustration when he asked me to help and I wouldn't do it. From my perspective, some of the times he asked me to help were because he was more focused on getting last minute invoices out to his customers for the business he was working to rebuild, watching television, or waiting until the last minute to begin working on assignments. I found it funny at this time how now he wanted my assistance, but when I was working on my masters and doctorate, it seemed to me that he would never take the time to read over something if I asked, or even take an interest in what I was doing. As I started to think about it, that hurt. I felt like I was always pouring into him, and always pushing him, and always wanting what was best for him, but I found it difficult to remember the times when he poured into me.

As I sat back and began looking at my husband working full-time and taking evening and online classes, I began to feel some type of way. I felt like he never supported me the way that I was supporting him, but was he to blame? Maybe I was to blame because I never spoke up about it. Being "Ms. Independent" when I reflect on it now, maybe I had the attitude then that came off as I can do it all by myself. This was a time in my life where I was beginning to question myself more and more of whether or not marriage was for me—as I was losing my joy.

CHAPTER 6

Mustard Seed Faith

I grew up believing in God and joined my church when I was nine years old, but it was not until 2013 that I came to realize what faith was all about. At this time in my professional career, I had been promoted from assistant director from one program to the director of another within the university where I am employed. Then unexpectedly, as a result of the resignation of my supervisor, I had the opportunity to be promoted once again to assistant dean. With every opportunity for advancement, I sought the approval of my husband. Though he said he supported me, his actions and words shown made me feel differently. He seemed to complain about my commitment to my job and the long hours that I would work. I found this funny because now that the shoe was on the other foot, it didn't seem to feel so good. Work for both of us had become consuming and the time that we did spend together didn't focus on us as husband and wife, but as parents to our two children.

Work was honestly consuming me; I was becoming frustrated with the demands of my new position and the fact that many of my colleagues who had become close friends were leaving the institution put me in a place of wanting to leave myself. But on November 12th of that year, God spoke to me in my office, and He said, "Trust Me." I grew up in the church and I had heard of people hearing the Lord's voice, but I didn't think I would ever hear it until he was calling me home! At first, I thought it was my imagination, but something truly came over me, and then a song by Richard Smallwood began to play on my computer and the choir sang, "If you will only trust me, trust me, trust me." I realize then that God was gradually preparing me for my life ahead.

I didn't tell anyone what I had experienced that day, and I was actually still questioning myself as to whether or not I had really heard God speak to me. When I left work, I had to stop by the grocery store, and as a result of what had occurred, I went down the spice aisle and bought a container of mustard seed. Throughout life I had heard my pastor and others speak about mustard seed faith, and to remind myself of what happened, I taped a mustard seed on my work computer the next day.

With the new year upon us, and getting acclimated with my new position, I was still frustrated with my home life, and at times I felt like I wanted a divorce, but we somehow survived to celebrate our eleventh anniversary in 2014. Things weren't perfect, but we were working to be a family, and now expecting our third child! Not in a million years would I expect to have to relive something similar to what I experienced with my first pregnancy, but I did. I continued to question God as to why this was happening to me. I didn't understand what I was doing to cause my husband to have to seek the attention of others. The only thing that I could see myself being guilty of was working and pouring into others, and I would come to realize, those were the issues.

We were going through the motion as a couple, but it felt more like we were roommates and parents than husband and wife. Both of us were working ourselves to death, but it seemed like we could never get on one accord with one another. We had never jointly shared our finances—his money was his and my money was mine. We rarely saw eye to eye and we rarely did anything together at this point in life. This continued on until 2017 when I felt like I couldn't take the pressure of life anymore.

CHAPTER 7

Midlife

That year I began to see a counselor. I knew things were getting to a point that I needed some help, and I wasn't comfortable with talking to friends and family. I had seen counselors before in life; one time while in college when I suffered from depression, and again while suffering from postpartum depression with my firstborn. I reached out to a big sister of mine from church and she recommended someone to me. I will never forget her response to me, "Lisa's good, but she keeps it real." Then she proceeded to laugh. This was exactly who I needed, because I knew deep down inside that I had to do some serious soul searching or I wouldn't survive—mentally.

I made an appointment to meet with the counselor, and I can remember her saying to me that I seem to be "together." When I meet people, I always try to present my best self because I believe first impressions make lasting ones. I could tell from our first session she was just who I needed to help me during this time in my life.

This year was filled with moments that I would later realize were confirmations from God as to where he was leading me. In March of that year, I told myself that I was going to start doing things for myself again. As I reflected, I truly lost myself in my marriage. I became a stranger to myself. I would look in the mirror and cry, not knowing who this person was on the other side. I poured so much into my husband, children, and others that I didn't realize I was completely empty. Each year, the university holds a scholarship gala, and as an administrator I feel obligated to attend, and each year I would ask my husband to attend with me. This particular year, however, I ended up attending by myself. I had asked him in advance, and he agreed to go, but as usual, his work schedule that day caused him to back out at the last minute. As I was putting the final touches on my makeup and hair in the bathroom, my oldest son came in and said, "Mom, I love your new hair color." When I turned to smile, tears began to form in my eyes. I grabbed him and hugged him so I could wipe the tears away behind his back, because I didn't want him to see me cry. I was hurt. My little boy would complement me when I desired the same thing from his father. At this moment I reflected on the words my husband once spoke to me that I thought I had buried but realized was actually festering: "I'm not attracted to you anymore." Since hearing those piercing words a few years ago, I didn't know what I had done for him to be so numb to me. I didn't know if it was me not keeping myself together or just us content with one another because we had been together for a while. He seemed to never smile or look at me as if he was attracted to me even now. I had reached a point in my life that I just wanted him by my side—for comfort though uncomfortable. For many activities and events that I was involved in, to include church, we rarely shared in them together. Sometimes I would not take part in things because I knew he would not want to attend. I got so discouraged at one point, I stopped attending church. I was tired of people asking, "Where is your husband?"

I realized at that point in my life I would have to create a new normal in my life, which would require me to do some things for myself without him. My first opportunity would occur that spring as I committed and began planning to attend a reunion cruise with my sorority sisters. At my counseling session before the cruise, I remember telling my counselor that this year would be the year of change for me, and so it began as I made plans to celebrate my twenty-year reunion with my line sisters. It was going to be a stretch at the time, for me financially, but I knew I needed this getaway to begin processing my inner thoughts that were silently killing my heart and mind. That April, eighteen women would reconnect to celebrate with each other and engage in some eye-opening conversations that I never imagined. This trip, however, would be the first that I had taken away from my family for more than an overnight stay, and anxiety was beginning to kick in for me as the time approached. When I traveled for work, it seemed to me that my husband became disturbed. A night or two before it was time for me to depart on a work trip, he seemed to become more distant and irritated by me. I never could understand it, because I would always make sure things associated with the kids and the house were covered in a way that his schedule would not have to be altered. I would have my mom, my in-law(s), or friend assist with the kids, and I would ensure that the children's clothes were prepped, and meals in order before my departure. I tried to avoid travel as much as I could because of how he came off to me, but I was not about to let this deter me from celebrating with my line sisters.

This trip was much needed. It allowed me to remove myself from my normal of work and family and allow me to enjoy me. This was my first experience with true "me time" since marriage and motherhood. At the culmination of our reunion, we took part in a rededication ceremony that would forever change my life. I reflected on the words based upon Christian principles and knew then upon my return I would have to continue to evaluate my life as my fortieth birthday approached in July.

It seemed like each month now, something would happen to jolt me and my emotions. The following month I spent the afternoon with three of my dear friends—Jackie, Keisha, and Marilla; we were just getting together to catch up. I made a call to my husband that day while hanging out with my friends at Jackie's house, and I don't remember the full conversation, but I do recall that he was out cutting grass for a customer. As we talked, he seemed to snap at me, and I remember responding that he was acting just like his father. When I said that, he lost it with me. I don't remember what was said, but I do remember the tears welling up in my eyes and me doing all that I could to save face in front of my friends. But I failed. I broke down as they tried to comfort me. I was hurt, angry, and frustrated. I never talk about my marriage to anyone, but today would be different.

I told my crew I didn't think I could take it anymore, and I wasn't sure I wanted to be married. I didn't believe in divorce, but I was miserable, and I didn't know what else to do. They comforted me and encouraged me, but not once did they impose their feelings on what I should or should not do—those are true friends. From that day forward, I remember limiting my interactions and conversations with my husband. I didn't know what to do, but I'm glad I realized at that time where I needed to return—and that was to church.

It seemed as if the devil was doing all he could to prevent me from getting to church each Sunday. Even if I tried to get things in order the night before for me and the kids, something seemed to happen and I would be at tears, but I would push on. I was yearning for answers because I was not sure how much more I could take. I always heard that the Lord would not put more on you than you could bear, and I was trying to understand how much more I would be able to endure before breaking. In my late June counseling session, I remember recounting Father's Day evening with my counselor. I spoke to her about how I had planned dinner at Mickey and Mooch's for my husband and the conversation we had about our relationship. Though he may not have meant it in a hurtful manner, how he described me pierced my heart. He said that he would compare me to a pickup truck, because I was reliable. It took all I had to hold back tears as I sat across from him at the table in silence—numb. I told my counselor that some changes had to take place in my marriage because I was at the point of giving up. I told her that I was going to make sure that the trip to the beach for my daughter's dance competition would be filled with family activities, and I would plan a birthday getaway with just my husband to take the steps to try to change our relationship, and to see if we could rekindle the flame that once glowed.

I worked to mask my pain in front of the kids on the beach trip a week later, but I was miserable. I was worn out from just the dance competition alone, and every time I tried to do something as a family, my husband seemed to want no parts of it. I know the beach was a place to get away and rest, but it was also intended to be family time away from the house. That July I planned my birthday trip to visit my close friend, LaKeeva, and her husband in Norfolk, Virginia. It afforded us time to talk and reflect and laugh for a change. It felt good, but things still didn't seem right. What I was doing didn't seem natural. For a long time in the marriage when I looked in my husband's eyes, he didn't seem happy, and my perception caused me not to feel happy. I was coming to the realization on this trip that we had truly grown apart. I truly began to accept that I was living a lie and wondered if he was doing the same.

On August 1st the bible verse that appeared on my phone said, "Be still and know that I am God." (Psalms 46:10 [KJV]). That startled me, and I took a screenshot to capture it (and I still have it this day). What was God trying to tell me? The academic year was about to begin, and we would return to even less time as a family and be consumed more with work. So, I prayed, and I did just that, waiting on God to lead me.

CHAPTER 8

Lord Of The Harvest

I can remember the month of September 2017 as if it was yesterday. I was about to return to my home away from home to celebrate my line sister's fortieth birthday. Everybody knew that if you lived within a certain radius of Chapel Hill, you better be in attendance or you may be disowned! I have grown to love and respect my line sister, Anitra. One thing is for sure from my perspective, she has always lived her life—period. This is one celebration that I did not intend on missing, especially with all that I was feeling personally.

I drove to Chapel Hill on Friday, September 8th and planned to use the day as a time to reflect on some of the best years of my life. My first stop, of course, was at Hinton James, the dorm I stayed in my freshman and sophomore year of college. I toured other spots on campus before I headed to Durham to meet a few of my line sisters. As usual, when I get with them, I get a sense of peace and comfort, and our conversations always give me an honest and genuine perspective by others on life. And life only got better that evening when we met others for karaoke. Saturday was spent at the UNC vs. Louisville football game reconnecting and running into classmates and having lunch with a few of my line sisters on Franklin St. We wrapped up the weekend by partying throughout the night with the birthday girl. I even grabbed the mic and sang with the live band! It was just like old times and I felt alive and that I could truly be me without wearing the mask to cover the pain I was actually feeling inside. Being around my close friends and engaging in conversations about life and marriage made me eager to want to return home and continue to give mine another try.

Sunday morning, I made the trip back home early because it was my mother's birthday and my husband had intentions of cutting a few yards. I wanted to make sure I got back in enough time to take the kids off of his hands and to have brunch with my mom. When I arrived in my garage, I took a moment to pray. I asked God to be with me as I returned to the house and I prayed that I could move forward in my marriage. As I opened the door from the garage, I was greeted by my children. They are always happy to see me when I return (and usually because I am bearing gifts). I hugged them, grabbed a banana for my youngest who said he was hungry, and proceeded to go upstairs to unpack. When I entered the bedroom, he was propped up watching television. I went alongside the bed to give him a kiss and asked how he was doing. He informed me that he had hurt his back the day before, and I asked why he had not told me. He responded that he was ok and didn't want to disturb me while I was enjoying my time away. A few seconds later my youngest enters the bedroom with a banana, and all I hear is my husband's agitated voice fussing at me, "Why did you give him a banana?! He isn't going to do anything but make a mess with it!" In the blink of an eye, my will to fight was gone, unbeknownst to me, for the last time. I didn't say a word. I turned and walked to my closet to empty my luggage, but really to hide the tears that were streaming down my face. I went to the toilet closet to buy more time to get my face cleaned up so no one would know the sadness on my face and the pain in my heart.

Trying to stay focused on my plans ahead and collect myself, I went in the kids' rooms to find them clothes to wear for me to iron. As I pulled out the ironing board in the bedroom, I was questioned about what I was doing. "Why are you ironing clothes?" he asked. "We are going to brunch to celebrate my mother's birthday," I reminded him. "You just got back from being out of town. You need to rest," He responded. Now he knows good and well I am not going to miss being with my mom on her birthday. I told him that I would rest later, but right now the kids and I would be going to brunch. I could feel his frustration with me, but I wasn't changing my mind. I got the kids dressed and we left to meet my mother, father, and brother at a restaurant close by.

I tried to pretend like everything was well when we arrived. I hugged both my mom and dad, then helped the kids to get seated. I had to get myself together, so I walked outside of the restaurant to see if my brother had arrived. When I walked out the door, he was parking his car. As he approached me, he could tell that something was wrong and asked what was going on. A lump was in my throat and I couldn't speak, but the tears began to stream down again. I said, "I can't do this anymore." My brother asked, "Are you talking about your marriage?" He was actually experiencing the same thing, and he said to me, "If you can fight for it, fight for it." In my eyes, but unbeknownst to my family and friends, I have been fighting for years, but I feel like I no longer have the strength or heart to go on. When we went into the restaurant all I saw were my kids—they would be the only reason that I would continue to stay the course.

My daughter's birthday was three days later, and we would have dinner but planned to celebrate her birthday with her friends the upcoming Saturday. That day started off as usual. I woke her up and wished her a happy birthday, helped get her along with her brothers ready for school, and dropped them off. I headed to work so that I could get some work done before I would return to her school to bring cupcakes for lunch. To my surprise, when I arrived to her school, her godfather was driving up and had balloons to celebrate her day. She was excited to see the two of us, and even more excited for the cupcakes! Though I was smiling on the outside, I was sad on the inside as I continued to reflect on the state of my marriage. How much longer could I continue to suffer inside? Could my children tell what was going on? Did God still want me to be still? What should I do?

As my daughter's godfather and I were returning to our cars after lunch, I spoke up and said, "I don't know if I can do this anymore." He didn't know what I was talking about. I began to tell how I didn't feel loved, supported, or wanted. You could tell I caught him off guard because of his facial expressions, but you could tell he knew I was serious from what was reflected back at him. He didn't say much, because he was my husband's best friend, but like everyone else, he encouraged me to hang in there.

Driving back to work, all I could do was stare in disbelief. My mind began to reflect on all of the birthdays that had been celebrated for the kids at school, and I was the one who was always there to make it happen, and even on this day, the kids' godfather showed up. Then I began to question myself. Do I do too much? Am I overcompensating for my kids? Am I making a big deal out of nothing? I couldn't understand why my husband never made the sacrifice to celebrate the kids, and always focused on the fact that he had to work. Well, I work too, but I figure out how to make things happen that I feel are important for everyone—including him. I was tired. I was empty. I was at wits end. Then the unthinkable happened.

CHAPTER 9

Signs

B efore I headed home from work, I reached out to my husband to figure out where we would eat for dinner for our daughter's birthday. We would decide between two of our family's familiar spots when I made it home after work. As I turned into the neighborhood my anxiety began to kick in. This had begun to happen since the summer, and I didn't know how to stop it. As I drove into the garage, I said a little prayer as usual, and proceeded to enter the house. As I walked up the steps, I was greeted by baby girl. "Happy Birthday, sweetie!" I said as I hugged and kissed her. She thanked me and proceeded to follow me down the hall. Then she said, "Momma, the water is off," as I just walked across the threshold of our bedroom door. I know I looked at my husband with piercing eyes. I said nothing, and he didn't either. I bee lined to my usual retreat—the closet. *What the hell*?! I am thinking to myself as I am working to gather myself and not show my anger in front of my daughter.

Now, my husband and I had discussions previously about ensuring bills were paid on time in order to avoid interruption. I never could understand why he wouldn't talk to me if he needed help with paying something, and if the water was off, that means more than one payment had to have been delinquent. The last time it happened I told him that if it ever happened again, I would leave. Now that was not the only reason. Between the issues with infidelity and delinquent payments and utilities being interrupted and many other situations and circumstances that should not have been overlooked, I had to give an ultimatum and stand up for myself. Maybe the water had been cut off this time because of a break or something going on in the neighborhood?

He didn't say anything, and I just gathered everyone up so we could head out to dinner. Very little conversation took place at the table. We engaged with the kids about their day and their activities but said nothing to each other. When we returned to the house, I just couldn't be there. While he headed outside to mess with the meter, I made sure the kids were prepared for bed, and I told him that I was going to run to Walmart to pick up some items. I don't really remember the drive, but I do remember sitting in the parking lot and googling signs of divorce. I wasn't surprised at all when I realized that we had all the signs except for physical abuse and drug addiction. As I walked into the store, I sent the link with the signs to my husband via text message. His response made me feel like he had no regard for my feelings at the time. He said, "You just need to come home so that we can make up in the bed and forget about this." *REALLY*! I thought to myself. We barely communicate, better yet get intimate on a regular basis. I truly could not believe his response, as I walked around the store dumbfounded, dreading to head home.

As I returned to the house and entered our bedroom, with an unexpected peace and calmness I said, "We need to separate." The next thing I know he is packing some things and approaches me as I am in the bed on my phone. "That's the problem right there! You're always on that phone!" Yes, I thought to myself, I am always on the phone. Usually, now, I am on my bible app, but outside of that, I work to talk to others about my college and opportunities for adult learners to begin or finish what they started as far as a degree is concerned. Why? Because my job and that of others rely upon the enrollment of individuals in our college, and I definitely am committed to do all that I can to make sure I market the program so that I, of all people, do not lose my job, and in all actuality, my job gave me validation of my importance, which I didn't feel I received from him, but there was no need to even waste my breath trying to explain. It was too late. I was officially done.

The next few weeks would be days of just going through the motion and avoiding interaction as much as possible, pouring myself into work as usual and getting my kids to school and their activities. I so needed to escape, and for the first time in my life, I went with what I felt like doing—I ran away. Friday morning, I got up as usual, got myself and the kids together for the day. I dropped them off at school and I decided to just drive. I drove until I reached one of my favorite places in the mountains. I checked into a hotel room and just sat. For the first time in years, it was just me. No husband, no kids, no work, no parents, no responsibilities, no planning, no suitcase—just me. I sat in the room and just listened to my mind run. There was so much in it and I couldn't shut it off. I remembered a book that I read, *The Seed: Finding Purpose and Happiness in Life and Work,* which spoke about releasing what is in your mind, because our thoughts clutter our minds like weeds. So, I grabbed the hotel notepad off of the nightstand and just began to write whatever came to my mind. Some of it was coherent and then other stuff was random phrases, statements, and thoughts. When I couldn't write anymore, I began to cry. The tears would not stop, and for the first time, I didn't have to make them end or hide them. I released freely. That cry was so exhausting, I just crawled in the bed and slept.

When I awoke, I figured I better let my husband know that I would not be home. So, through the preferred choice of communication, I sent him a text and let him know that I was out of town and I would be back in the morning. For the first time in the longest, he seemed to be concerned about where I was and why I was there, but I was too drained to try to explain via text. He continued to send text messages and even attempted to call, but I just responded that I was safe, and I would be back the next day. Guilt began to set in, but I worked to fight it. I had to get away for me.

A few weeks later I would have another opportunity to still away, but this time to homecoming at my alma mater. I returned to "blue heaven" on Friday morning, giving myself an opportunity to once again reminisce on some of the best years of my life. I immediately connected with one of my former roommates and college friends and we laughed and caught up about the latest happenings in our lives. I always felt like me around my Carolina family, because I was just Laura, not wife, mother, daughter, sister, or dean. An amazing time was had that Friday night. I'm known for taking selfies and "usies," and I don't think I missed a photo op with any of my classmates, but who would have ever thought that one photo could ruin the remainder of my weekend.

Saturday morning, I was awakened by a call from my husband. He was not a social media user, but someone had sent him a picture from the night before. "Who is that you are all up on in that picture?!" I responded, "What are you talking about?" He responded, "I don't like that picture!" Again, I asked confused, "What are you talking about?! I took pictures with everyone!" Then I received a screenshot and replied, "Oh, that's just a guy from my childhood that I hadn't seen in years." He responded, "Well, you need to take that down. It doesn't look good." Trying to avoid confrontation by phone in front of my classmates, I conformed to the request. I really could not believe that he was really upset over a picture! What was really going on? Trying not to focus on the fact that I felt he was being accusatory, I prepared to attend the homecoming game and post-cookout at a classmate's house, only to have the remainder of my afternoon ruined with conversations of going back and forth about what I was and was not supposedly doing. It took all I had to hold my tears back in front of people. I finally stole away and cried. I was beginning to get tired of crying, and something had to change upon my return home. And it did. This was the season of harvest, and I would begin to gather what I needed to bring about change in my life.

CHAPTER 10

November

Weight is something that I have struggled with in my adult life. To be quite honest, I stress eat and I love food! As much as I know that certain things that I eat aren't good for me, I indulge in them anyway. I have gained and lost weight over the years, and regardless people comment, "You aren't big," but inside I feel and look otherwise to the most important person—me. In September 2017, I began a journey to change my physical appearance by incorporating physical activity and eating healthier, but things came to a halt when I injured my knee in November.

It was a Saturday, and I went for a jog out of anger and frustration, because though I had communicated that we needed to separate, we were still residing under the same roof. I recall taking a step and feeling a sharp pain shoot through my knee. I was too far from home to turn back and too hardheaded to call and have my husband to pick me up. So "Miss I had a child without an epidural" decided to endure the pain and continue on her route. When I finally got home, I lay on the living room floor on the rug on my back. My knee throbbed and I could literally feel my heartbeat in it, but as usual I sucked it up and made my way upstairs to the shower. After bathing, all I wanted to do was relax and elevate my leg, hoping to alleviate some of the discomfort. After only a few minutes, it began to swell. I attempted to get up to go eat but I couldn't walk, let alone put pressure on it.

For the next few days, I would hobble around enduring the pain, and even experienced my knee buckle, almost falling on multiple occasions. After ignoring the injury for a few days and the side-eyes of family and co-workers, I went to see a sports medicine doctor and found out that I tore my meniscus. As a result, I had to change the intense workout I was now used to and only take part in low impact activities, which bore me. This caused me to stop my daily workouts with my personal trainer. I felt defeated at this point and gave up on working out altogether.

Struggling with both mental hurt and heartache, I had to get away from the house. I wanted to do something with my children, and they asked that I take them to the movies. We decided to see the movie *Wonder*, and I cried uncontrollably at one point in the theater. My oldest son looked on and asked if I was ok. I told him, yes, even though I wasn't. The movie made me think a lot about myself. I have done a lot of things in life for others, working to fight my true feelings—hurt, sadness, anger—for the benefit of others to gain or be happy. I wish I could be selfish; I wish I didn't care so much. I really did want to just be happy, but as usual, I was concerned about the feelings of others.

As I sat in the theater, I began to wonder if I may have married for the wrong reason(s). Getting married freed me from my parents, and specifically my dad who had high expectations of me, and that came with a great deal of pressure, resentment, and pain. But as a result of how I was raised, I have always strived for perfection; not to *be perfect*, but to do what's right and decent. and also to please others, such as the case with my father. Throughout my marriage I was referred to as *perfect* many times by my husband. I couldn't help that my goals, aspirations, and expectations of myself and anyone I associated with were sky-high. However, my husband seemed to interpret this as me attempting to be perfect, and I resented that. So, when I say I may have married for the wrong reason, I know now that I looked at getting married as freedom from my father and the resentment and pressure that had built over the years.

All that I knew as I peered over at my kids sitting to the left of me in the movie theater, was that they were the one thing keeping me in my current situation. Their well-being is very important to me. Therefore, I wanted to make sure we got help for them before we did anything that may be detrimental to them. I didn't want them to think that momma didn't love them. I didn't want them to feel that they were the cause of this transition. I was miserable and just wanted to run away. I wanted to care for my kids and just be alone. I wanted to find myself and be at peace. I was tired of feeling taken for granted.

It was the Saturday after Thanksgiving, and I wanted to get into the spirit of Christmas early. Christmas is always the time of year that makes me feel good on the inside. With all I was struggling with internally, I could use some joy. So, we began to put up the Christmas trees and decorations. Things felt different this time. I sat back and watched my kids as they trimmed the tree in the living room, and I held back tears, wondering would this be our last Christmas all together. Then a few days later, I took cupcakes to the daycare to celebrate my youngest child's birthday, and again, as his father sat beside me, I wondered, what would this time next year hold?

CHAPTER 11

The Power Of I Am

It finally happened. I reached my breaking point—I reached rock bottom. I felt like I was literally suffocating. Anxiety had taken over. I couldn't breathe. All I could do was cry an inconsolable cry. I couldn't sleep. My mind was wondering. That night I rose up from beside my husband in the bed for the last time and walked to my daughter's empty room. I didn't know what else to do but to fall on my knees and pray. I realized that I could no longer hide or wear a mask. I needed to be saved, and there was only One who could do it.

That next morning, I reached out to my fellow Carolina classmate and friend, Michelle, and told her how I was feeling, but not specifically what was going on with my marriage. She recommended that I read *The Power of I Am* by Joel Osteen. I gathered up enough strength to put on clothes and drag myself to the bookstore to purchase it. Instead of returning home, I decided to go to my parents' house and sit in my childhood room and read. This book would FOREVER change my life and begin my restoration process as I began a new spiritual journey in life.

That same day, my dear friend, Clifford, from college, had a pep talk with me. He reminded me that I couldn't let my circumstances get me down. I must remain the confident person that I am. He said talking down to myself and depression weren't a good look either. I am so thankful for good friends who "checked" me and didn't let me feel sorry or guilty.

I believe confirmations come in threes, and I received yet another unexpected sign I do believe was ordained by God. On this particular day I received a Facebook Messenger notification from another college classmate, Kimberly Joy Morgan. The notification spoke of a life coaching opportunity, and she asked me to let her know if I was interested because she would love to have me. I responded that I would love to join. She then inquired as to how things were going for me. I told her I was doing fine. To be honest (at that moment) I was doing fine. I told her that I was confident about some decisions that I have made and that I would be moving forward with them in 2018. I continued sharing that I knew things wouldn't be easy, but I am strong, and I am a child of God, and I am a queen, and will live as so.

She responded, "I'm loving your attitude! Glad you are claiming your position and space! God has you, and you have support from many. Let me know if I can help in any way." Her challenge to me to take advantage of this opportunity was timely. I told her that I had to trim a lot financially because of my transition in 2018, but I would be prayerful and let her know before the deadline as to whether or not I would take part. She followed up, "Don't let financial issues stand in your way. I work with anyone that has the want to. We'll find a price that works for you and I'll set the payment there."

I told her, "I receive it." I began crying tears of joy. I was embracing my current situation and learning to accept what friends had to offer me. Where I have been embarrassed or too prideful to receive or ask for things in the past, I was learning to be humble and appreciative of now.

"I'm so thankful you were honest! You see, I only accept six women in the program because I hunt for women who want it! Some let pride, money, or laziness get in the way—others speak up! I'm excited for you!" she messaged.

I replied, "I have let pride get in the way too long. I am humbling myself to become the best me in the moment. I am deciding to take off my mask of sadness, hurt, and disappointment. I know I am freeing myself from my marriage. I am scared, but I am fearfully and wonderfully made. I know God has me . . . He knows my heart, my mind, and my soul. I am strong and going to walk into my new season. I am my daughter's role model, and I am doing what is right for me."

"Amen, Laura . . . it's so hard to come to those realizations and act on them, but you know the truth, and so does God. Walk in the FULLNESS of who He created you to be," my friend said.

I replied to her, "Yes, it truly is . . . especially when you worry about what others have to say." For the first time, I began to open up about the possibility of divorce. "I know this was hurting my husband, and I would never intentionally hurt him. I just couldn't continue to live unhappily. I have tried for years to get us into consistent counseling, to attend marriage retreats, read books together, read inspirational quotes together . . . I have worked on things alone and prayed, but we just co-parent. I had been feeling emotionally neglected for a while, and it was impacting me negatively. My self-esteem was at an all-time low . . . enough was enough! I was going to get my life back. I was pouring into myself because I had been on empty and just going through the motions because I thought that is what I had to do for the rest of my life."

She responded, "Your transformation is going to be unbelievable because of your readiness! I know you would never intentionally hurt him . . . and I also understand the hurt you lived in for years . . . it's a really tough place to reside. I've coached quite a few people in this area of life and you'd be surprised how you will both come out better, if you are willing to do the work. I know how hard it is as a Christian woman too. There's a lot that goes along with that . . . just know that NO one has walked your path or in your shoes so stand firm and know you sought God on this decision."

I replied to her, "That's what I want him to understand." I then shared with her that I was reading *The Power of I Am*. She shared with me that she had the book and had twenty-three I AM statements that she reads over her life daily. She exclaimed, "Can't wait to dig in with you in 2018!"

I thanked her so much for the time she shared with me that morning, and I told her, "Count me in, please." She replied, "You got it! Pray about the budget and get back to me . . . we will set a price that makes you comfortable." I responded, "Will do, and again, thank you." She replied, "You are welcome and enjoy your week!" I replied, "I AM! You too!"

Christmas Eve I made a conscientious effort to get to church. I had not been regularly attending, but with all I was going through, I knew it was necessary. As I attended the 9:30 a.m. service, Pastor Jones, Senior Pastor of Friendship Missionary Baptist Church, where I have attended since I was five years old, preached the sermon *Beyond These Things*. He spoke from John 21: 15-17 (KJV) and how Simon responded to a feeling of fear—he was afraid of (an) action. Simon never answered if he loved Him (God) more than these things. He never responded to the quantitative love of God. Pastor continued to speak about how this is a human response, and how the Lord wasn't asking a "feel" question, like how do you feel, Simon? Then he reminded the congregation that "So as he thinketh in his heart, so is he . . . Simon did the best he could with what he had, but there was something the Lord was looking for...there was something beyond." Pastor Jones then made reference to a book, *How God Changes Your Brain*. "This book," he shared, "is about compassion. Sympathy compared to empathy: sympathy is what you feel; empathy is emotional, mental. Compassion goes a step further than empathy . . . it allows us to be more tolerant of others." At this point in the sermon, I felt like he was speaking directly to me and all that I had been toiling with inside. I knew this message was confirmation for me. 2018 would definitely be a season of change. I would focus on taking responsibility for myself, no longer allowing things to just be, for my life was worth saving.

CHAPTER 12

Entering Into The New Year

A few years ago, my sister, Keisha, told me about a book called *The Seed: Finding Purpose and Happiness in Life and Work*. As referenced before, in this book the author spoke about the importance of clearing our minds of thoughts. Many times, we have so much inside our heads, it becomes like weeds and we become weighed down. With all that I was processing in my life, I felt it was important to start journaling to clear my mind and to process things that were actually occurring in my life. Who would have ever thought these entries would clearly reveal the path that my life would take for restoration, specifically the days leading up to the New Year?

Since reading *The Power of I Am*, I began awaking each day and reading devotionals, journaling, and spending the first moments of each day with God in prayer and meditation. I grew up in the church and believed in God, but something had begun to feel different in my life. The day after Christmas I awoke and immediately began to pray my "I AM" prayer. I tried to stay in bed but felt the need to get up. I grabbed my phone and saw my Bible app verse for the day, Isaiah 41:10 (KJV), "Fear thou not, for I am with thee: be not dismayed; for I AM thy God. I will strengthen thee: yea, I will help thee; yea, I will uphold thee with the right hand of my righteousness." Then I saw a plan in the Bible app related to this verse from the book *Don't Settle for Safe* by Sarah Jakes Roberts. The devotional for the day spoke of NO MORE EXCUSES. It spoke about how living a life prepared for the worst possible outcome is like living in a cage—it's not freedom. This is how I have felt. I had a mindset that I always had to prepare myself for with thoughts like, *Oh Lord, what is going to happen now?* I haven't really felt, or had the ability to live and focus, on the possibilities of the "what ifs." As the plan said, I have always talked myself out of the good things God has promised to all who live according to His purpose. Following the plan, I decided in that moment that I will not settle for a life dictated by insecurities or previous experiences. I have access to power that is capable of working within me to free me from any mental and emotional bondage that has convinced me a better life is not within my grasp. I cannot tap into the power and hang on to excuses at the same time. My heart, my mind, and hands must be free to lay hold of all that is ahead of me! Similar to that which I read in Joel Osteen's book, *The Power of I Am*, I have to shed the excuses, which is a discipline that I must practice with my thoughts, communications, and actions. There is only language that declares: I WILL! The daily devotional series from Sarah Jakes Roberts reminds me that I must learn what stopped me in the past. If the challenge to heal and become whole was issued by people other than myself, then my journey will always require permission before progression— CONFIRMATION. I will not let my destiny be determined by a democracy, and I will avoid the temptation to make my healing contingent on approval and validation from other people.

All of this aligns with what I tell my students, "Speak into existence your dreams and aspirations, and step out in faith to achieve them." Words are powerful. But not only do you have to speak them, you must mentally believe and also work at them—with no FEAR. And I thought to myself that my fear can be conquered by **F**acing **E**veryday **A**rmed and **R**eady! And again, this is where learning the "I Am" affirmation statements came into play. I AM . . .!

Wednesday, December 27, 2017

The scripture for today: "But those who hope in the Lord will renew strength" (Isaiah 40:31 [New International Version]) This is definitely timely. There are a lot of changes that are about to take place in my future, and I will definitely need strength to stay forward, focused, and following God. Forward, focused, and following—those are some words from a sermon spoken a few years ago by my dear friend and former youth pastor, Reverend Y. Trevor Beauford. They have always stuck with me. I am grateful for where I am today. I've been through too much not to worship Him. God has kept me even as I have tried to navigate my own life without seeking His direction. I believe, as a result, I have suffered more than I should have, and that's what happens when you don't walk by faith but by sight. I have shut off everything important to me, and most importantly God, because of the hurt, pain, and frustration I have masked. I endured it because I allowed it, but where I am now had to happen, as heard through a sermon by Steven Furtick, Pastor of Elevation Church. This is my Malta (a reference from the sermon). After watching that sermon, I then watched one by Bishop T. D. Jakes, Pastor of The Potter's House where he said, "You Can't Get Over Anything That Hurt You Until You First Give Up What You Had in Mind." This spoke to me as Bishop Jakes spoke about capacity. From the sermon I began to realize how large my capacity is to love but may not have been matched, and how as a result I have possibly closed up my heart to everything and walked around like a zombie—missing blessings because I haven't allowed things to flow naturally.

I am flowing again this morning. I am receiving the word God is giving me through various means, and I am seeking joy and positivity instead of worry, as to whether or not what I am doing is for me. I have sacrificed entirely too long and as this morning's sermon "Never Waste Your Feelings on People Who Don't Value You" from T. D. Jakes states, "Success comes with sacrifice." Because of the sacrifice over the years, I forgot my own value. God paid the ultimate price for me. He gave His only begotten son. I'm more valuable than silver and gold—but I forgot. I let what I was going through diminish who I am and whose I am. I lost myself and haven't been me for years. I am getting my life back with no regrets!

In my daily devotional *Don't Settle for Safe*, by Sarah Jakes Roberts, she asked "Have you ever taken time to consider your own emotional pattern? Those that create recurring emotions and therefore yield habitual actions. Ask yourself: Why did this happen to me? What did it teach me? How do I keep it from ever happening again?" What is going on in my life happened to me because I allowed it. Part of it was me being naïve and part of it was just being vulnerable and putting too much trust in man. This has taught me that I come first and foremost. I have ignored the signs over and over again. I failed to put my (oxygen) mask on first. It is so true. I have always put everyone else before me—NO LONGER! And that is how I must keep it from ever happening again. As the devotional reminds me, I must find the root to what is blocking me from complete joy. Lately, my husband has been saying that he thinks I'm vulnerable (meaning that I will let anyone get in my mind and do anything, as if something is wrong with me and I'm not stable), and now I see that he was right. I am vulnerable with God and myself, working to release the negative in my life and focus on the positive and joy. God's plan for me includes joy, peace, and love. Therefore, I must remain forward, focused, and following to receive all of it.

Thursday, December 28, 2017

Today's devotional from *Don't Settle for Safe* is entitled "Live Your True Identity." This is exactly what I am working towards. I am no longer masking who I am, what I need, what I want, what I desire, what I aspire to become. I am no longer conforming to what others need me to be or what others expect me to be. God created me in His image, and I am fearfully and wonderfully made—I AM ME! As the devotional reminds me, "I can't take life into my own hands. I must control the part of me that believes I know better than God. I must trust that if I don't have something it's because I am not ready for it. I believe that if it's on my plate I can handle it. I will stop doubting my strength and testing grace. I won't do what feels right; but do what makes me a better person. I can do all things through Christ. I am capable and I am worth it.

Another reading for today entitled, "A New Start" from *Don't Look Back* by Lisa Singh states, "Holy Spirit, help me from today to live my life with a view of what is ahead; help me to stop looking back!" I have been living beneath the truth that Jesus died on the cross for me to have a new start, even today, and because somehow the lie of my old life seems to envelop my soul. Also, from the devotional, Jeremiah 29:11(KJV) says, "For I know the thoughts that I think toward you, saith the Lord, thoughts of peace, and not of evil, to give you an expected end." I am letting go of the past and walking into each day—forward, focused, and following God's plan for me.

Friday, December 29, 2017

Today's devotional from *Don't Look Back* by Lisa Singh stated that looking back is a heart condition and referenced Proverbs 23:7 and Luke 12:34. The devotional reminds us that our heart was made to follow the ultimate treasure, which is God himself, but only Jesus could give us the heart to understand that, and without this understanding, we will end up chasing treasures of this world which are of lesser value. Like Lot's wife, I keep looking back over my life, not realizing all that

God has in store for me ahead. God said, "Look not behind thee, neither stay thou in the plain." (Genesis 19:17 [KJV]). The devotional reminds us that in the moment of having to leave behind people, possessions, and relationships we hold close and dear to us may seem like the most difficult thing to do. But when you put your trust in the one who knows best, the present pain will eventually turn into the greatest gain in life. The truth about looking back constantly and living in the past is that it will drain the very life from you. I prayed, "Holy Spirit help me today to leave the past behind and lead me to an abundant life ahead."

Sunday, December 31, 2017

Today's entry focuses on the 9:30 a.m. worship service where Pastor Jones spoke from John 21:24-25 and John 20:30-31. The sermon, "You Can't Tell It All, So Tell What You Can" referenced the book *Live Your Dash* by Linda Ellis. The scripture from John said never let your life be regulated by human stuff. Pastor asked, "In your ordinary circumstances, do people see Jesus in you? You can be alive and lifeless." Then for the evening New Year's Eve Service, Pastor Jones spoke to the message, "God's Got It— God's Got This." The passages referenced were Psalm 8; Psalm 89; and Psalm 145. Pastor spoke about how the writer raises some questions and gives us some affirmations. We are told that too many of us are miserable. He said, "If you don't want to praise Him, I'll take the rocks to praise Him," as he references one of the texts. Pastor encourages us to look up a little more this year. Look beyond our personalities and positions. Focus on God and remember God's got it! We need to have that "child faith"—like we see and hear when kids sing "He's Got the Whole World in His Hands"—they believe it! He further encouraged us to not give permission to devalue who you are . . . don't allow your body permission from giving God praise. Think of God's goodness instead of the negative.

I realize that I can't win this battle alone. Time is filled with swift transitions, and I must hold to God's unchanging hand.

As I take time to look back over the journal entries for the last few days of 2017, I realize that only God could have ordained the devotionals, sermons, and scriptures that were aligned with me preparing for the New Year, new beginnings, new mercies, and new opportunities and new blessings that He had in store for me. The journey ahead would make it clear to me how He works EVERYTHING for my good.

CHAPTER 13

The Year Of Confirmation

It has been almost four months since I told my husband we needed to separate. I am not sure if he didn't take me seriously, but I prayed to God that He would speak to me and assure me that I have done all that I could do in my marriage. I was trusting and believing that God would literally direct my path during this year, but I knew only He would be able to restore me.

It was the first day of 2018, and a verse I read during my morning devotional said, "Behold, I will do a new thing; now it shall spring forth, shall ye not know it? I will even make a way in the wilderness, and rivers in the desert" (Isaiah 43:19 [KJV]). I was already feeling and seeing a new thing happening in my life, in my heart, and in my mind. I had not been at peace and happy for many years because I tried to be in control of things on my own. I strayed from God; I allowed myself to avoid church because of the hurt, frustration, anger, and resentment. That was all the more reason that I needed to return to my roots and ground myself spiritually, resting my heavy burdens upon Him who is strong when I am weak. I suffered way too long, but I refuse to anymore. Each morning I am choosing to seek God first in my day and moment-by-moment throughout my day. I am making time to focus on the Word that will fill and lead my heart. I am a child of the Most High God—I am a queen and I am no longer allowing ANYONE to devalue me.

Usually on New Year's Day I am watching sports or beginning to take down Christmas decorations if I had not already done so. This particular morning, I viewed a sermon from Pastor Steven Furtick from Elevation Church entitled "It Is What It Is, But It's Not What It Seems." As with the devotionals from the past week, I felt like he was speaking directly to me. I can remember him saying, "You might be the one that God uses for a bigger purpose." This stuck with me as I took notes in my journal. He continued his sermon by talking about faith, and how some people don't exercise faith because they live in denial. They begin to use their faith as a cop out and don't confront things for what they are. That "they" that he continued to speak about felt like me. Then Pastor Furtick stated, "You can't get over what you do not own!" My toes at this point had been crushed, not just stepped on.

Though I began my day with prayer, devotion, and the sermon, the day ended up being extremely stressful. With the little interaction that we had during the day, I felt like my husband really needed someone to help him through his past because it was negatively impacting his current life, which included me. Again, I felt like he refused to hear me when I communicated with him and I continued to feel trapped and cornered and I had had enough! He avoided confrontation at all costs and acted as if things would just work out if they were left alone. I needed to get away because I refused to let the kids see me continue to cry because of my unhappiness in our marriage. I didn't want them to sense negativity between their father and me because we must co-parent, regardless of the outcome of our marriage.

When my husband and I were newly married, I remember taking a trip to Texas for work, and we arranged for him to travel with me. One evening we were poolside and I communicated to him that I felt like he had a wall built up with me, like he could not wholeheartedly open up to me. I felt like he loved me but was reserved and cautious with how much he shared with me. For years, I still felt like he could not let his guard down with me. I believe my gut was right when I said it was a result of him not knowing his birth father. At this current time in my life, I was focused on seeking God for confirmation about things from my past and present, and He in fact confirmed what I always felt was a barrier wedged between me and my husband.

Even during this time in my life when I had informed my husband that we needed to separate, I still had compassion for him and truly wanted resolve for him and confirmation for me.

An NFL playoff game was on that Sunday evening, and I don't know how the discussion started, but I asked my husband if he wanted to find his birth father. To my surprise, unlike his responses in the past, he said yes. The first time that I asked him about his real father is when we were preparing invitations for our wedding, and I asked if he was going to send one to his father, and he said no. I was not really aware that he didn't have a relationship whatsoever with him. Another time I asked him about finding his father was when I was pregnant with our first child. Being a new mother, you want to know everything that you can that may impact your baby in any manner. Every time you go to an appointment you are asked about family history, and I could never give clear answers as far as my husband's side was concerned. An attempt was made to contact his father at that time, but persistence didn't get us any closer to who the person was. However, this time, things would be different.

Within two days, God revealed to me that someone who had been my mentor for almost nineteen years may have possibly been a connection to assist with the search, and it turned out to be a perfect connection.

A week before we were scheduled to meet my husband's birth father, I attended a personal counseling session that went well as usual. I talked to my counselor, Lisa, about how I felt like I slowly died on the inside during my marriage. I spoke about how I was so focused on my husband and trying to understand him and please him or get some type of reaction and affection from him that I almost treated him like a god. I also spoke about being empty, similar to a car. The gas light can come on stating that you are on "E," but I told her I was beyond empty, and actually felt more like a car broken down on the side of the road. Her response gave me assurance that it is ok for me to be feeling the way I do. What was more surprising—downright shocking to me was her next response. She stated, "I want you to think about conducting a seminar this summer for women. You would be amazing!" It caught me off guard but was actually confirmation. A few others had stated the same thing, but I had always downplayed what I was capable of doing. I thank God that I am a new me and I am going to move on this request. I recalled something that I learned at a conference, "Sometimes people can see things in you that you cannot see in yourself."

When I got home, I felt drained from the session and needed a lift. I began to listen to music and then was led to view a sermon by Pastor Steven Furtick entitled "Why Am I Anxious?" This sermon recapped the last two weeks of my life—further confirmation from God that He has a purpose and plan for this journey I was on. As I reflected on the sermon by Pastor Furtick, I recall him saying something like, "You're not an option, you're a privilege." This is exactly right. I believe (again) that I am special. I am fearfully and wonderfully made. I am a queen. I am beautiful. I am smart. I am intelligent. I am a precious jewel, and to have me is definitely an honor and a privilege. I have truly been lost in my marriage—walking around empty with a mask on, not feeling worth anything and feeling nothing special about myself because I was relying on my spouse to pour into me. I didn't feel he was pouring into me, and so I would seek fulfillment by pouring into my children and anyone else who would make me feel special. I have lost so many years as a result of not turning to God with my burdens.

The next morning the *3-Minute Devotions for Women* spoke about sleepless nights. Many years of my married life had been consumed with worry, fear, anxiety, so many weeds in my head that I didn't rest. My mind and my body have been so tired because I didn't take my burdens to the Lord and leave them. But as I have begun this new journey, my mindset definitely changed, and I am truly understanding how significant having faith just the size of a mustard seed could have such an impact on my life. We must think it, so we become it. We must speak things into existence. But most importantly, we must speak life over ourselves. Therefore, I no longer go to bed with negativity. I pray that God releases it so I may go to sleep in peace—and I believe it. I no longer worry, and I have been getting the best rest in years.

There's a story in the bible about Sarah. It says, "As for Sarai your wife, you are no longer to call her Sarai; her name will be Sarah . . . I will bless her so that she will be the mother of nations; kings of peoples will come from her," (Genesis 17:15-16 [NIV]). Similar to Sarah moving from "I am a failure" to "I am a Princess," everything began to change for me too. I am confident, I am happy with myself. It's like I've been born again—renewed. I am Laura again. I have not felt like myself in many years. I have been a wife, mom, daughter, sister, dean, and everything else to everyone in need, but not me, Laura. I am happy to be back! I cannot reclaim the lost time, but I'm happy joy has been restored in me. There was a time that I could not figure out how to find the good in things; my life and mind became consumed with negativity. But I ran across a scripture that said, "Praise be to the God and Father of our Lord Jesus Christ, who has blessed us in the heavenly realms with every spiritual blessing in Christ" (Ephesians 1:3 [NIV]). This was found one morning in one of my devotionals. The passage asked if it was possible to respond with praise when our earthly life appears to conflict with spiritual truth? I was realizing that yes, it is, because the spiritual truth may bless us or be used to bless someone else. In another reading from the Bible app was a series entitled: "Help Me! I need to change my life!" by Pastor Brian Houston. The topic for this particular day in the series was "Obstructions to Change." It stated that some people want the fruit of change, but they don't want the discipline of change. Change, as it states, requires a process of transformation in renewing our mind—you have to change the way you think, and it must align with God's word. This is what has started occurring with me, and it makes me think of the scripture from Proverbs 23:7 (KJV), "For as he thinketh in his heart, so is he . . ." On this particular morning, something out of the ordinary happened. My husband asked me to read this devotional with him. I shared with him my thoughts that change is inevitable, however, for change to occur the mind, body, and spirit must be aligned. I could not recall the last time we prayed together. As a matter of fact, I could not recall him ever praying for me when we were together. The only times would be the few where he may have said grace. This was somewhat of a bittersweet moment, but truly uncomfortable because it definitely was not familiar.

With all that was going on I felt my mind changing. My daily routine was now focusing on God's word in the morning and focusing on my life at present and in the moment, not in the past, or tomorrow. Clarity and confirmation come from being focused on Thee. Taking the opportunity to focus on the word allowed me to make connections and have a positive outlook on the day. It also allowed me to make connections with what is going on in my life and it equipped me with what I needed to have a positive outlook and to see things through. Taking time throughout the day when necessary to say a simple prayer kept me focused in the moment and provided me with a redirection to make it through the day. And at night my prayers allowed me to truly rest. I learned to pray and release anything that was keeping me from my peace so that I may rest at ease. Prayer still works and I'm glad about it.

The next day we would set out to meet his father. My prayer at midday was: "Dear Heavenly Father, I thank you for this day. I thank you for my life, health, and strength. I am grateful for my family, my friends, my colleagues, my students, and my job. Lord, I pray that You will continue to keep watch over us as we complete today's journey with tasks and events seen and unseen. Lord, as we prepare to meet my husband's biological father for the first time, let your presence and power be known. Allow all of us to act, react, and interact in a way that is pleasing to You. Lord, if it is your will, please allow this encounter to provide peace and understanding for my husband and be an opportunity for his father to release this burden he has been carrying for forty-four years. And Lord, if you do not see fit for this to occur, please continue to guide and direct our hearts, minds, and bodies until contentment and understanding are resolved between these two individuals so that they may continue on the paths you have prepared for them moving forward. These and all other petitions and blessings I ask in Jesus' name. Amen."

That evening we were unsuccessful with the search, but we came in contact with another individual who would be the connector for my husband and his birth father to eventually meet. A few days later we got in the car as a family to officially go meet his father for the very first time. As my husband buckled his seatbelt, I asked him how he felt and he said, "I'm excited, nervous, apprehensive, happy, sad; all those emotions I feel right now. Every emotion you could probably use to explain something, I am feeling right now." That night, a new chapter would begin in my husband's life, and confirmation would be provided to me. He met his biological father for the first time, and as a spectator, the encounter seemed to be perfect in God's time and ordination. I am grateful to have been able to help orchestrate this reunion. As a friend of mine reminded me, I was able to give my husband something no one ever did or would ever be able to do.

When we returned from the introductory dinner, my husband drove the car into the garage, and I asked him, "So how do you feel?" He responded, "I don't have any more grudges about anything. I feel like a wall has been torn down." This was a bittersweet moment for me. As I got out of the car I worked hard to keep a smile on my face, because I was happy that he was in a good place now knowing who his father was, but I held back the tears that confirmed to me what I had felt for so many years.

This occurrence brought things back into perspective for me. Even though I was happy for my husband, the pain in my heart resurfaced. As usual, I put myself on the back burner for him, and put on hold my innermost feelings. Though fighting to help him with internal peace, I was neglecting my own. The wall that was built up and prevented my husband from truly letting me into his heart and life would be the same wall that would crumble that night, but only time would tell if we would be able to pick up the pieces to bridge our relationship.

CHAPTER 14

Momentum Not Motion

It was evident through my daily devotionals and live or YouTube sermons, that God was speaking to me. Reflecting on them since December, it became obvious to me that EVERYTHING GOD ORDAINS. There is no other way to explain how the readings, lectures, and messages aligned with my life and situations.

For years I let what was not said to me get the best of me and make me feel unwanted and less than. This caused me to question who I was and to lose myself, right in my own home. I was depending upon someone else to give me confirmation instead of knowing and believing in myself. I thank God I am finally beginning to see—again—who I am and whose I am. Watching T. D. Jakes's message "New Year, New You" on December 25, 2017 he quoted Romans 12:1-2 (KJV), and what stood out to me was ". . . be not conformed to this world but be ye transformed by the renewing of your mind, that ye may prove what is that good, and acceptable, and perfect, will of God." I realized that I had conformed to this world; I was doing everything that I thought was expected of me and was more worried about what others would have to say.

Transformation at this point in my life was inevitable. God had begun to renew my mind. He was showing me that the mind is a powerful thing, and in order for me to walk in my truth, I would have to begin with my mind—change my thinking. I had to know who I was, regardless of how others may have made me feel. I am responsible for me, and as my husband once told me, "I cannot make you happy. You are responsible for your own happiness." When he initially said that to me, I was hurt. I didn't understand. I mean, I thought a husband and wife were supposed to bring happiness to one another. Now that I reflect with a new perspective, he was right. I am responsible for my own happiness, and I had to get my life back. This was not going to be an easy process, and I definitely would not be able to go through it alone, but it would be critical to have the right support along the way.

I received another message from Kimberly Joy Morgan reminding me about her offer to take part in life coaching sessions with her. With all that was happening, I failed to follow up. "Hey love!" she said. "No pressure, but the group is getting ready to gear up to go! There is still one more spot if you feel God has this open for you. Please let me know by the end of the day. Thanks so much!" With no hesitation for the first time in years about how I was going to fit this in my budget, I responded "I'm in!" The very next day I received my welcome letter to Momentum Not Motion 2018. In Kimberly's words this group would allow us to do LIFE together for the next 12 months. Kimberly Joy Morgan was definitely a Godsend. This woman who was once just a classmate from college and within my circle of friends, would become one of my closest confidants and prayer warriors in my life.

After taking part in my first Momentum Not Motion session led by Kimberly, I was excited about the possibilities. I knew that God would provide me with confirmation about the group through a message—and He did. I viewed a sermon one evening by Pastor Steven Furtick titled "My Confidence is Coming Back." (I'm sorry y'all, but at this point in my life, there was no doubt in my mind that God was ordaining EVERYTHING I did and was providing confirmation to me for reassurance.) Furtick preached:

> "The devil cannot take your calling, so he attacks your confidence
> . . . Christian confidence comes from: (1) your conscience (the mind),
> where the presence of God is and (2) community. You need some people
> in your life because of the temptation to turn back . . . You have to follow
> Christ for yourself, but you can't follow Him by yourself. God brings
> people in your life that surround you and help your confidence."

It was clear that God was not only working on my thoughts, but he was working on my tribe. I read a devotional entitled "Consolation Amid Conflict" and the scripture was from 2 Corinthians 7:5-6 (KJV). "Our flesh had no rest, but we were troubled on every side; without were fightings, within were fears.

Nevertheless, God, that comforteth those that are cast down, comforted us by the coming of Titus." It was clear that God was bringing "Tituses" into my life for the journey ahead, and Kimberly was definitely one.

It was evident that I was growing spiritually while trying to determine where my life was headed, or should I say where my marriage was heading. One particular morning at the end of January, one of the devotionals spoke about how words are like seeds. "Keep thy tongue from evil, and thy lips from speaking guile" (Psalm 34:13 [KJV]). It went further to say that my life will move in the direction of my words. I look to the Lord for wisdom. As I journey on, I want to make sure I make wise choices in my life because my choices impact me and others. He knew my heart and knew what was best for me, and I know He gave me this scripture and every other one in His perfect timing, for He knew the plans He had for me.

Throughout my marriage I was careful with the words that I spoke to my husband, because I knew once something was said it could not be taken back. I never ever wanted to intentionally hurt the man that I loved. However, my idle mind had me to reflect on words that were spoken to me. The man I thought the Lord had kept for me told me he was no longer attracted to me. When he spoke those words, it crushed me. I truly believe now that was where our marriage had begun to take a turn for the worse. When he stated that to me, I took it and didn't respond. I didn't know what to do. I had taken these vows with this man and had committed to be with him for the rest of my life, for better or for worse 'til death. But he wasn't attracted to me. Those words stayed with me and any time something wasn't right, they always came to the forefront of my mind.

Reflecting back on all that I have been through, it was time to walk in my truth and speak my peace. From this moment forward, I was committed to speaking with respect and honesty. I had to determine for myself if it was truly time for me to accept that this season in my life was coming to a close. I realized that I had honestly been miserable for years, but I was always afraid of what others would say or think if we were no longer together. I was miserable for years from feeling ignored. I was miserable for years feeling neglected and not appreciated. I was miserable for years from feeling taken advantage of. I was miserable for years from him coming home late at night with no explanation other than he was hanging out with his friends. Did I communicate all of these things and more to him? Yes. Did I think he would eventually change? Yes. Did I try to read books and work on things that I controlled? Yes. Did I try to get him to go to counseling with me? Yes. Did I try to get him to read books and articles with me? Yes. I never thought in a million years I would reach a point to even think about divorce, because of the vows I took between him and God, but in my heart, soul, and now my mind, it was time to make some decisions.

Once again, I wrote in my journal that I was going to work to mend my marriage harder than I ever have. I don't know how in the world that was possible, because from all that I felt I had done, there was nothing else that I could really do. I do know now, however, that my spiritual walk was much different this time, and I knew that this time God would provide confirmation as He was already doing.

Since communicating to my husband in September that we needed to separate, nothing had really changed in my perspective, except for me. Since that time, he seemed to be like Dr. Jekyll and Mr. Hyde in my eyesight. One day he was sending me text messages that spoke of him keeping the kids from me if I followed through with the separation, and then other times he was begging and pleading with me to give him another chance. All in all, we were still moving as if we were roommates and not soulmates. We were cordial but careful, looking as if we were really trying to avoid one another. The one thing that we did work together on was supervision of the children. I asked him if he had found a place to move, but that always seemed to go on deaf ears, so since I was still paying the mortgage, I decided that I would move into another room. He didn't seem to be happy with this, but I wasn't doing something for him for a change; I was doing it for me.

With all that was going on, I expected to see something different in his responses and actions towards me. One morning when I had to travel for work and he was preparing to leave for the day I said, "I'm leaving for work today," but as usual, I received the same dry response. "Ok. I'll talk to you later," he responded. No, "Drive carefully, be safe," and no "Call me when you get there." At that moment, I prayed to God and stated that I was trusting Him to guide my heart, my mind, and my soul, no matter how difficult things may be ahead.

That night while sitting in the bed in my hotel room, crying, I was glad to be alone and free to feel the way I was feeling. At home, because of the children and being afraid of them seeing me cry and asking what is wrong, I worked to wear the mask. I wondered how separation would impact them now and, in the future, individually and collectively. I would smile though I was dying inside to avoid getting a look of "What now?" from my husband.

I had just finished watching a video of Lisa Nichols as part of my homework, which I referred to as "life work," assigned by my life coach, Kimberly. In the video Nichols COMPLETELY REVEALED WHO I HAVE BEEN FOR TOO LONG. She said I am my rescue—no one else! It is so true. No one can save me, but me, and I was so glad that I began the process of restoration. So, the nerd I am googled the word restoration, which was defined as the action of returning something to a former place or condition, the return of a hereditary monarch to a throne, a head of state to government, or a regime to power. I am returning to my former conditions, who God created me to be and not what I have allowed myself to become. I am returning to the hereditary monarch, because I am not only a queen, but a child of the Most High God. A friend of mine reminds me all the time that I am a queen. I had completely forgotten that and lost myself along the way in my marriage.

As Nichols said, "Most people want the convenience of transformation without the inconvenience that comes with it." I realized that is what I have wanted. I was definitely experiencing that now. I have to come to grips with the fact that this restoration of myself is necessary, and with this transformation, some people may be hurt, but it is definitely not my intention. But there I go again, always worrying about and putting others before me. Nichols goes on to say, "The doorway is for you to go through—but you're trying to take everyone with you." As a wife and mother of three, this restoration was going to have an impact on my family, but I am no good for anyone else if I'm not good for myself. "The world is following my example of how I treat me," Nichols commented. I realize that I am better to others than I am to myself—but no more. I have been holding on to my family and using them as my excuse for not having time, money, energy and everything to be the best me and become who I am destined to be and accomplish my goals. But now, I am ready to love people from a distance, if necessary. As Lisa Nichols states, "I have to celebrate, forgive, and commit to myself." I must start running from someone else's dreams harder than I run from my own. I have mistaken spirituality for self-development. I am glad to be walking in my new season of self-development, complimented by spirituality.

When I researched self-development, I had a flashback to college, as Maslow's Hierarchy of Needs diagram was pictured ("What is Personal Development," (Maslow, A. H., 1970), Motivation and Personality (2nd Ed.) Harper & Row, NY, https://www.skillsyouneed.com/ps/personal-development.html). Maslow (1970) suggests that all individuals have an built-in need for personal development which occurs through a process called self-actualization. Self-actualization refers to the desire that everybody has to become everything that they are capable of becoming. In other words, it refers to self-fulfillment and the need to reach full potential as a unique human being. For Maslow, the path to self-actualization involves being in touch with your feelings, experiencing life fully and with total concentration ("What is Personal Development," (Maslow, A. H., 1970), Motivation and Personality (2nd Ed.) Harper & Row, NY, https://www.skillsyouneed.com/ps/personal-development.html). But even with self-actualization, I have to have my spirituality because my feelings are associated with my soul and doing what is right and what is best for me. Who would have ever thought that a work trip would allow me such a breakthrough? As I prayed and prepared for bed, I realized that by taking care of myself would make me seem as if I had a big ego, which is what I feared others would think, but it was about what God's big plans are for me, because EVERYTHING GOD ORDAINS (E.G.O.).

That night I made a commitment to myself to truly work to walk by faith and not by sight. I was so grateful for my assignment from my life coach and the insightful video by Lisa Nichols. God was truly moving in my life, and I had to keep my focus on becoming the best me so that I may break the cycle of going through the motions for everyone else but instead live in the moment for me. I prayed that God would allow me to be an example to others of how to live vulnerably, but true to me, and not worry about what people have to say.

The next morning when I rose, I received an unexpected text message from my husband. It included a devotional from a bible app plan and a video attached. I'm not sure what the devotional stated, because I didn't capture it in my journal, but it mentioned the words "You will prevail." Those words speak directly to the transformation that I have begun to go through. My official record for my restoration began December 22, 2017. I began to claim that day as the day that I began the work to return to the real me; the one God created me to be, the one who has been lost, the one who has been lifeless, the one who has neglected herself, the one who poured out and into others and not herself . . . and beginning THAT DAY, I would live with no regrets.

I have said and heard, "speak your peace," but not until now have I fully processed it. I have not spoken my peace for fear of how others may feel or react, instead of speaking my peace so that I may be in peace with myself. Instead, I have suffered and internalized things that have eaten at me to my core and filled me up with negative—resentment, regret, anger, sadness—but no more. I cannot get back the time that I have lost not living the true me, but I can be restored and move forward living my best life (and I wrote that before I heard Lil Duval) for me and no one else.

This transformation and course along life's journey for me has and will be trying, unsettling, and scary, but when I put my focus on Him, my anxiety, fear and frustration will go away, or at least improve. Change is inevitable, and I'm glad about it. I am coming into a new me that is bolder and stronger and confident. A devotional for this particular morning referenced I Samuel 17:37 (KJV), reminding us that the Lord will go with us and be with us in all that we do and go through. Along my journey, I have to know that God will give me the strength for every challenge and battle. I have to know what is best for me, and as the devotional from Joel Osteen, "Prophesy the Right Thing" states, "The heart of the wise teacheth his mouth and addeth learning to his lips" (Proverbs 16:23 [KJV]). I have to also prophesy—speak into existence—the right things in my life, and I must not allow others, not even my husband, fit me into what they want me to be or become.

I also realize at this time that my husband, too, was going through a transformation as a result of me speaking out about my feelings and walking in my truth. My friends were going through a transformation because of the open discussions and interactions we are engaging in privately. God has moved me to begin telling my story, my testimony through a book and seminar, and other platforms, thus, this book was birthed—*Restore the JOY: A Transformation Through Confirmation.* The JOY, to hopefully use my testimony to help and save others or both. I'm thankful for the word and courage to speak my truth and face my truths head on. (Side note: Today is July 24, 2019. I am in Dallas, Texas with one of my line sisters, working to complete the book that I spoke about in my journal in January of 2018. This is occurring in God's timing, not mine. It took this long for me to fast and pray and receive confirmation from Him that this is His will for me to do.)

CHAPTER 15

See It Through

Ir's been almost four months since I sat down with my husband and told him we needed to separate. Since that time, and even now, I am working to convince myself that I have done all that I could and can do in my power for our marriage. I believe in marriage and never thought in a million years I would be in my current situation, but I am, and I must determine how to move forward. I can no longer depend on myself and my thoughts; I must now understand God's purpose and plan for me. For too long I thought I was in control, but I now know that I must be still and quiet and receive confirmation from Him.

This last Sunday morning in January, my husband was preparing to play drums at a nearby church. I told him that the outfit he had on for church was my favorite outfit of his right now. I realized that I had not complimented him or made such statements to him in a while. As he headed out the door to church with our oldest, he asked me to pray for us. He has never done that before in almost fifteen years of marriage. The former me would have blurted out, "I always do!" but remembering what I have been learning through studying the word and my devotionals, I was still and quiet.

It actually felt uncomfortable hearing him speak those words, because change is uncomfortable. As I sat on the edge of the bed with our youngest child sound asleep, and our daughter in her room sick, I thanked God for moving in him to take the lead to go to church with our oldest son and prayed that they both receive a word from the Lord that would be life changing. I prayed that their experience together may allow them to bond, that the Lord blesses our family collectively and individually, and that God may have His way with our marriage and each of us as individuals.

I have always wanted my husband to lead our marriage and our household from the beginning. I honestly lost faith in his leadership. I have had to play the role of the head of household out of fear and frustration, and I can't seem to let go of the position now. This may be why we are in the predicament that we are in now. But why do I feel that it is my fault because I wanted us to succeed and have more in life and not settle? This makes me so angry inside, and it is why I am working to step back and allow him to lead and see if any hope remains for us.

I'm truly turning over a new leaf. I wasn't feeling 100%, so I decided to take the day off. The old Laura would have sucked it up and talked herself into getting up and going to work, but this day I did what I felt I should do FOR ME. And how ironic, the devotional for this day spoke about the secret of contentment. The scripture in the *3-Minute Devotions for Women*, Philippians 4:12 (NIV), stated I have learned the secret of being content in any and every situation, whether well fed or hungry, whether living in plenty or in want. In this faith walk, I am truly beginning to understand that God knew me before I was in my mother's womb, and it is true that contentment is an inside job, and the secret to contentment comes from understanding that where I am now is exactly where God wanted me to be. I have been at a low, and I must trust Him.

It has taken me a few years to finally get past the introduction of *The Purpose Driven Life*. As I read Day #3, I made notes in my journal about four points:

1. I am driven by guilt—I am running from regrets and have been hiding my shame; unconsciously punishing myself.
2. I am driven by resentment and anger—I haven't gotten over times I've been hurt; I've held onto it.
3. I am driven by fear—I grew up in a high control home and have been afraid to venture out. I have played it safe, avoiding risks and trying to maintain the status quo.
4. I am driven by the need for approval—I have allowed the expectations of others to control my life.

As I sit here reflecting, it is more than clear that as much as we may want to focus on others and the impact they have on our lives, the true focus is on ourselves and what we allow or do not allow for we only have control over our own actions and reactions. We make the choices that we have to live with. So, at this point I take ownership for all that I have allowed in my life—hurt, pain, disappointment, resentment, frustration, lack, heartache—everything. And at this point I truly realize what I learned in the spring of 1997 is true, "I am the master of my fate, I am the captain of my soul," as the poem "Invictus" by William Ernest Henley says. I cannot and will not allow anyone to prevent me from walking in my truth from this point forward. I will truly, solely depend on God to lead me along my life's journey. I will no longer conform to what others may want but will move with confirmation from what God has planned for me.

As I continue on with *The Purpose Driven Life* one of the chapters speaks about seeing life from God's view. It asked what has happened to me recently that I now realize was a test from God? What are the greatest matters God has entrusted to me? From the book *The Power of I Am*, Joel Osteen said that sometimes the reason a promise from God is being delayed is because of what we are saying. I realize now that I was so focused on my mate over the years, I didn't speak life over or into myself! I am supposed to pray for others and leave it in God's hands, but I was consumed, confused, and didn't know what to do. I couldn't understand why it felt like my husband couldn't love me the way I needed. I didn't trust God. If I had, I would have spoken life over myself, because I am only responsible for my actions, not that of others. I should have prayed for him and let it go. My pride wouldn't allow me to speak out about how I was feeling because I was so worried about what others would have to say, or maybe I wasn't really living up to the "expectations" of a wife. Many times, I felt worthless, but now I am seeing that all along God has been with me; I have just denied Him. I should have cast my cares upon Him. I know that my marriage has been a test for me. I am now in a different mindset, and I see the evolution. I am thankful that God has placed friends in my life to provide me with comfort in knowing that He is God, and I am His child, and I have the power to pour into myself when others don't, won't, or can't. God has entrusted me with my own life, and I must no longer look back, but remain forward, focused, and following His plan for my life.

When I began my daily ritual of rising first thing in the morning and reading devotionals and praying, I thought the readings were coincidental. However, I have come to realize that they are actually the power of prayer and God's will. Each day

I have realized that God is truly ordaining my steps and my path. On the morning of February 3, 2018, I was taking part in my morning practice and the title for one devotion was "Do Your Part" and the scripture was from Isaiah 43:19 (NIV), which speaks, "See, I am doing a new thing! Now it springs up; do you not perceive it? I am making a way in the wilderness and streams in the wasteland." It was true; He was doing a new thing in me and for me, and it was my choice to accept it and embrace it. The fact that life on earth is just a temporary assignment is changing the way I am living right now. As scary as it may seem at first, we live and must die, but the life we live determines our final destination—our eternal home. I must live the best life that I can, not worrying about others, but what God speaks to me to do. In this particular moment, after toiling with the title of this book, He gave it to me as I listened to John P. Kee's "Life and Favor." God is showing me He can and will RESTORE THE JOY.

CHAPTER 16

I Am Because Of The Great I Am

I have now been working with my life coach for over a month, and one thing she encourages me to do is to write "I Am" statements. These statements align with what I have decided to focus on. I must speak life over myself and believe in me if no one else will. I'm all I got! Not only am I all I got, but God is the great I Am, and I am made in His image. I am realizing that life and death are truly in the power of my own tongue, and I choose to live—again.

Not only have I been working with my life coach, but I had a personal counselor, and a marriage counselor that I was working with at this time in my life. The personal counselor was necessary for me to have someone independent to completely open up to about my most intimate thoughts. In one particular session, she asked me if I felt my husband would attend a session with me. I told her that I didn't know but I would ask. Well, for my next session, he did attend. We each shared a few minutes separately with her, and then she ended the appointment with just me. I already felt in my heart what she was going to say, but I still refused to accept it and continued to fight.

"You all are not equally yoked," she said. The words stung to actually hear, but in my heart, I knew that she was right, but I had to know without a shadow of doubt that this was true. But how would I know? My heart pounded and I was choked up inside. We walked outside and I asked him how he felt about the session. As usual, with little emotion, he shrugged his shoulders. I hugged him and asked what we were going to do, and his response was the usual, "I don't know." He continued and in a nonchalant manner said, "If we gonna work on it, let's do it, but I have to go cut grass." I don't know if I had just become so sensitive to everything, but that "but" resounded loudly with me. I learned that "but" negates everything in front of it, and deep down inside I knew this would be my last attempt to save what we had.

At the request of my husband, I stopped my sessions with my personal counselor, and we began to attend marriage counseling with a counselor of his choice. Marriage counseling was serious. We were able to open up and release some things. It was good to complete a questionnaire together and know each other's love languages, but like that "but" he had after the session with my personal counselor, I had a "but" about why he wanted to go to counseling now. Was he doing this now because I had stated we needed to separate and be a temporary fix as things seemed to be in the past?

My husband, brother, and close family friend started a business a few years ago together while each of them was still working their full-time jobs. My husband's full-time job was his lawn service and as it grew, he was unable to give full attention to his responsibilities for the business he had created with the others. As a result, it became evident to the other partners that he could not manage both, and one day they sat him down and had a discussion about him and the business.

I wasn't in the meeting, but things did not go well. All I know is I had a husband who was extremely hurt and upset, and a brother who I was torn between. However, as a wife, I chose to support my husband, which damaged my relationship with my brother for a time; but he understood that I was choosing to stand behind my spouse. I did eventually have a conversation with my husband about this and communicated how I felt he was wrong with the situation. I decided, once an offer was made, to take over my husband's portion of the business, because I knew that the business would provide an extra revenue stream for our household. I took over because I thought it was in the best interest of our family, but it actually turned out to be a blessing and a curse. As I worked as a partner, I felt that my husband was not supporting me but looked at ways to criticize what we were doing and how we were doing things. He no longer had a say, but seemed to have so much to say, and it was frustrating.

I agreed to take a trip to the beach with my husband as our anniversary approached. As much as I loved the beach, I truly had some inhibition about going. We had become very careful around each other, and for the most part, we only communicated well in the presence of our marriage counselor. This particular morning before we departed for the trip, everything came to a head. Before we hit the road, I had to make sure that things were in order for customers over the weekend, so I asked him to stop by the company's storage. When we arrived, I got out of the car and proceeded to check inventory and place paperwork in storage for the weekend delivery guys. When I returned to the car, I felt like unnecessary comments were being made. There were complaints about me having to come to the location and how it seemed to be unsafe. I became livid. How dare he have anything to say about what I was doing and where I was doing it considering that he dropped the ball with the business, and I was now part owner as a result. I spoke my peace for the first time in a long time. I spoke of how I was doing this for our family. I spoke of the many times he as my husband would let me venture out at night and seemed to have no care in the world, even when I would ask for help or for him to go with me. However, because of what I perceived as bitterness, he didn't want to have anything to do with the business, even if it meant helping me. This was definitely not a good start to our anniversary weekend.

There was silence in the car as we left the storage facility. As the radio blared, I picked up the book I was reading at the time, *Big Magic: How to Live a Creative Life, and Let Go of Your Fear*, by Elizabeth Gilbert. This was another book that I was reading as a result of my life coach. I found it ironic at first, but then realized that it, too, was ordained that I was reading this book and other books that were allowing me to awaken what was once lost and dead. As we traveled along the words on the page resonated with everything that I was feeling and going through. My soul had been waiting for me to wake up to my own existence for years. More importantly, I had to begin again to just say what I want to say and say it with all my heart. I felt then, just as Elizabeth Gilbert discussed in the book, I would have to write a book in order to save myself, to make sense of my journey and my own emotional confusion.

Confusion—that's what I was feeling as we rode along the long stretch of highway exchanging very few glances and almost no words. What were we doing? What was I doing? As usual, I knew that I had to try with all my might to ensure that I had done all that I could do for this relationship. When we arrived at the resort, I did something I have never done, I headed straight to the bar. I felt miserable and thought about if I was going to be able to have any fun. I would have to be drunk in order to do so. He was excited that I decided to have a drink; I knew though that I was trying to mask my true feelings of not wanting to be there. In my mind I wanted to be there, but my heart and soul were truly empty. In between drinks I would still away into the ladies' room and talk with my friend as to how this wasn't working, and I just wanted to get home to my kids. My friend encouraged me to keep trying, because I had to know without a doubt that I was all in.

That evening we tried to find the restaurant where we ate years ago on our honeymoon. We thought it was no longer there, but it had actually relocated across the street. It was surreal to be seated there—we had come full circle. Where it all had begun would now also be the end. This trip truly felt like a revisit to all the things we enjoyed together and the opportunity for us to experience them one more time. When we first met, I enjoyed shopping and I always asked him to take me shopping. This particular weekend, he finally did it. He took me to the outlets and asked me to pick out whatever I wanted. I tried so hard to seem excited, but I was truly hurting inside. I was grateful for the gesture and for the nice things that I received, but I felt hurt at the same time because he was trying to do things for me now.

The last night of our trip we found a restaurant with karaoke, because that was one of our pastimes when we first met. It was truly bittersweet. As I stood in the front of the room and stared at him, I belted out the words to "I Believe in You and Me" by Whitney Houston. This was the song that I sang to him at our reception. The song I chose specially to serenade him because it spoke to how I had felt for fifteen years of marriage and almost twenty years together. As I finished the song and went to take my seat with him at the table, the words of the song brought tears to my eyes and a lump formed in my throat. I thought about the words that I had just sung for what I felt would be the last time.

I thought I would always be the one for him, but that was not the case in our marriage. For there was evidence throughout that there were other individuals who he had relationships with, but I forgave him and gave second chances. I never left his side nor hurt his pride (so I thought) throughout our marriage. As long as we were together, I placed him on a pedestal and treated him like a king. He never wanted for anything; I always took care of him and covered him. Maybe I was a fool to do what I did and to love him as I did, but I realized I could no longer live in this manner. I was lost in my marriage, but now I was freeing myself so that I could once again live and love myself more than I loved him. The morning before we departed home, as usual I completed my devotional time. One of the readings of the morning was entitled, "The Time is Near" and it referenced Revelations 1:3 (NIV), "Blessed is the one who reads the words of this prophecy and blessed are those who hear it and take to heart what is written in it, because the time is near." That morning before heading home, we took a walk along the beach. As we held hands it was evident that things had changed. I could no longer live a lie, and where our lives began as husband and wife would now end as simply parents of three beautiful children.

CHAPTER 17

Make A Move

T hings were truly beginning to change for me, and I was committed to walking in my truth, no matter how difficult it would be, I would live authentically and not be ashamed of the decision I had made. We all have choices, and I chose to live how I had lived for years. I chose to stay in a marriage because I thought I had no other choice. I took vows between him and God, and from what others told me, divorce was not an option. He hadn't physically abused me, and though there was evidence of infidelity, I had chosen to stay in the marriage. I stayed because I was more concerned about others than myself. What would other people think? What would our family say? I was emotionally neglected, and I determined for myself that I was worth more than settling in unhappiness.

I had the opportunity to watch the sermon, "Dysfunctional Comfort" by Pastor Steven Furtick of Elevation Church. What I received from the message is that in order to really follow Christ, I must come out of my comfort zone. Pastor Furtick stated, "Christ did not come to make us comfortable. When you don't understand the function of something you are more than likely going to get hurt from something or break it trying to engage it. Without understanding your relationships, you can have hurt." He went on to speak about how we have blamed the enemy for our conflict, but in actuality to find your calling one must have to forgo comfort—come out of your comfort zone.

As miserable as I had become, I was now realizing that in order to restore my joy in my life, I had to get comfortable with the uncomfortable and step out in faith and not fear. I had to forsake the familiar. I decided at this point I had to begin removing familiar things and people in order for me to clearly hear and understand where God was directing me. So many people, including family and friends, were integral in our marriage. As part of my vows stated from Ruth 1:16 (KJV), ". . . Entreat me not to leave thee, or to return from following after thee: for whither thou goest, I will go; and where thou lodgest, I will lodge: thy people shall be my people . . ." Our friends and family knew us from the beginning and had seen our journey from their lenses, but as with most things, it was not as it seemed. I did not want to make decisions after hearing others' thoughts because who wants someone's marriage to come to an end? But I had to make some decisions, many difficult ones that only I would have to live with. And I would have to answer to only one other—God. So, I prayed to Him that He would remove all distractions so that I could hear Him. I asked Him to put people in my life at this time who would pray and support me in a neutral capacity, not imposing their thoughts but only offer up prayers of support.

No longer believing in coincidence, I knew He had ordained the message I listened to before going to bed this same evening from T. D. Jakes, entitled, "God Is Gonna Give You A Shift" This sermon spoke about how most people are living from a heart place and not a head place and he said,

> So engrossed with what the heart feels—*you will never win a battle if you're having a heart experience in a head battle. Telling the enemy how you feel has nothing to do with what you know . . . It is with the mind that we serve the Lord. A person who moves totally out of emotions will forfeit life because of feelings—not living the best life.*

This was me, but I knew I could not begin to move forward without being mentally strong where I had not been before.

It was evident that our relationship had run its course. I initiated a conversation with my husband stating that it was time for us to move forward with severing our ties. There was no more denying that we would have to go our separate ways. The one thing that had kept me in the marriage was the kids. I shared that I didn't know how divorce would impact their lives, but I could no longer live for others—not even them. After almost a year of contemplation, attending counseling sessions as a couple (and by myself), not seeing eye to eye, and seeking confirmation from God, it was decided it was time to inform the kids of our decision to separate. We agreed we would work together to talk to them, but that was not the case when the time came. That evening after work he called the kids into the family room and told them we needed to talk to them. As the kids gathered around, he said momma has something to tell y'all. As with most everything else in the marriage and with the kids I was expected to take the lead. I spoke to the kids and told them that mommy and daddy loved them with all of our hearts, and nothing will ever change that. Then I explained to them that mommy and daddy were not really friends anymore and that we would be separating. Before I could explain what this meant, he interjected and said, "Your momma doesn't want us to be a family anymore!" I was livid but worked to keep my composure in front of the kids. I followed up with, "We will always be family. Nothing or no one can change that; I will always be mommy and he will always be your dad. You will always be together." The kids didn't really have a response; I didn't know if they were ok with it or didn't quite comprehend what was being communicated to them. Without further conversation I asked the kids to go upstairs to their rooms so I could talk to their dad.

"That was not what we agreed to and that was wrong," I said, burning up on the inside. He said give me your hand, and I reached out. He then took the rings off of my finger. I turned away and walked upstairs because there was no way I was staying in this house one more night. As I was putting clothes in my suitcase, he came to me and tried to give me the rings back. I kept saying no and to just keep them, because it was over between us. He wasn't giving up, but I wasn't giving in. As I zipped up my suitcase, he placed them on top. I turned the suitcase over and allowed the rings to fall to the ground. As I walked out of the bathroom, he asked me to talk to him, but I truly had no words. My daughter entered the bedroom as I was getting my jewelry from my dresser.

"Momma, where are you going? She asked. "Mommy is going to a hotel," I responded. "I wanna go," she said. "Ok," I replied. "Let's pack you some clothes." My sons saw this and wanted to go too, but I told them that they needed to stay with their father. My daughter and I checked into a hotel. To her, it was exciting and like a vacation; to me it was an escape.

Escaping would become my new normal. I had to have some peace in my life, and in order to have that, but also not cause too much disruption to my kids' lives, I began staying with my parents. The kids were used to this, because sometimes when my dad was ill or my mom was traveling, I would stay at their home. Now that I was back in my childhood bedroom, I would reflect on what my dad told my husband when he asked for my hand in marriage. "She can always come home." Who would have ever thought that after almost fifteen years of marriage and almost twenty years of being together I would be facing divorce? As I stared at the walls, to my surprise, I wasn't emotional, and I couldn't understand why. I actually had a sense of peace and calmness, but I questioned myself about what I prayed for but was now experiencing. Why was I not crying? This second weekend in a row where I had awakened in my parents' home, I read the following during my morning devotional "Daughter, be of good comfort; thy faith hath made thee whole; go in peace." (Luke 8:48 [KJV]). I realized in that moment that I had cried so many tears throughout my marriage in silence and behind closed doors, and now I was receiving what I had prayed and asked for throughout the years . . . peace.

Now that I had peace, I had to work to maintain it. A conversation was had about how we would go about co-parenting, and it went rather well. I could not recall the last time that we had spoken without it ending in an argument and misunderstanding. Still feeling some guilt, I didn't want to disrupt my children's lives, so I would get up by 5:30 a.m. at my parents' house, and drive to my house so that their father could leave for work by 6:30 a.m. This was exhausting, but it was the choice that I made for my children. After work I would continue to pick up my youngest from daycare and assist the others at home. I would stay around for dinner, and when it was time for them to go to bed, I would depart for the twenty-five-minute drive to my parents' house. This was taxing on my body, but it brought me comfort and peace of mind.

As I was preparing our luggage the morning of our family spring break trip, the scripture associated with my morning devotional came from Proverbs 4:23 (NIV), "Above all else, guard your heart, for everything you do flows from it." My heart had experienced a lot of pain and disappointment even when I tried to love, but I had to begin to love myself again. I also started the book *Abundance Now* by Lisa Nichols. As I read the foreword, it spoke about how many of us have something similar that threatens to stop us, and we realize that we have to do something to step out of lifelessness and step into greatness. It also said, "Don't resist the transformation that's on deck for your life." I truly know that I have to allow God to order my steps so that I may walk into my new season of peace and whatever else was yet to come.

As with all other trips, I planned the final trip we would spend with our children. On Easter Sunday I awoke in Washington, D.C. in the bed beside my daughter and my youngest son. This particular morning was different. I thought about how Jesus paid the ultimate sacrifice so that I may have abundant life, which includes expectations of prosperity, health, and other forms of fullness of life when faced with adverse situations. I felt like I was beginning a new life and living in the moment with no regrets. As usual, God gave me confirmation through the message on this Sunday that I watched on livestream. My pastor spoke about how you can't appreciate being up until you've been down. I had been down for a while, but God was giving me an opportunity to live again, and for that, I am grateful. I will continue to praise Him and find the positive in all things, for I was realizing that He had and was continuing to work everything for my good.

CHAPTER 18

Rest

"Come unto me, all ye that labour and are heavy laden, and I will give you rest. Take my yoke upon you and learn of me; for I am meek and lowly in heart; and ye shall find rest unto your souls. For my yoke is easy, and my burden is light."
(Matthew 11:28-30 [KJV]).

It was one o'clock exactly in the afternoon, and I finally decided to dust off the rough draft of this book and begin to write again. I have put off writing because of frustration, anger, fear of offending, and fear of hurting, but now it's necessary. Healing can't begin or truly take place if you don't release your feelings. I also heard Bekah Baker, author of *Built to Break: When God Writes Your Story and All Hell Breaks Loose* at my life coach, Kimberly Joy Morgan's Fiercely Feminine Conference say, "You must reveal in order to heal."

Thursday, April 12, 2018 began like a usual workday for me. I woke up and did my normal routine for getting ready for the day—morning meditation and devotion, which I had done for 103 consecutive days now at that point, taking care of my hygiene, ironing the kids' clothes for the day, and awaking and assisting them with getting ready for school. As I got two of them off to school, I decided to call a close friend to see if we could meet and I gave her a book she had requested. When I called, she was somewhat in a rush and couldn't meet, but took the time to talk to me. She did not realize how much I needed that. This morning I was feeling like I was reverting to my old self.

For some time now I had been walking in my truth and being authentic. Similar to the words of Dr. Seuss, "I said what I meant, and I meant what I said. I knew those who mattered wouldn't mind and those who did mind really didn't matter." Or they could not at least accept that I was in a transformation phase of my life.

As I was leaving the daycare to drop off my youngest child, instead of turning right to go to work, I decided to turn left and return home. I just felt like I couldn't do it today. I didn't have the strength that I have had many days in my life to push through, to put on a mask, to grin and bear it. My emotions began to take over. My eyes became filled with tears, the lump in my throat appeared, my temperature rose, and my heart began beating fast. Though no one was in the car with me, I just wouldn't allow myself to release what I was feeling. But when my eyes became too full, tears began to stream down my face—RELIEF. Why don't I allow myself to just be?! Why don't I allow myself to just feel?! Why do I think I must be so strong?! Why do I think I must be perfect?! As my friend and I continued our conversation, I told her that I was going home, and I just couldn't go to work today. Being supportive, she agreed that was probably best. As I entered the garage, I realized the notification would be seen by my husband on his phone, and I didn't want to be questioned. I hoped and prayed he would not reach out to inquire about why I was home. Maybe he would just think that I forgot something and wouldn't pay any attention. I don't know if he was trying to respect the boundaries I had set about giving me my space, but he didn't reach out to me as he normally would have.

I wanted my bed, the bed I had not slept in for months now. I wanted to truly be able to cry, be alone, and sleep without any worries or interruptions. As usual, before I could settle down, I had to calm my working mind. I pulled out my phone and checked to see if there were any pertinent emails that needed my immediate response. I texted my coworker and informed her that I just couldn't do it today. Because of our relationship outside of the workplace, she could tell something was wrong. She asked, "What do you need?" I said, "I need to cry and just be." "I don't think there is anything pressing at work today." She responded, "Go find some peace." At that moment I was getting in my bed and tears began to run down my face again. She sent another text, "I think you should call your counselor. You seem more depressed today. I responded that I didn't want to go to my regular counselor. I actually had not had a counseling session with her in a few months. The last time we engaged in conversation, she was telling me that I should be happy with the fact that my husband was evolving into the man I wanted him to be. But that was an issue I had. Why was he evolving now? Now he was becoming the man who I expected him to be after I told him we needed to separate. Why should I be happy now? This was a slap in my face to me! Whose side was she on? One session she is telling me I need to put my big girl panties on and put him out (which the thought of that scared me to death), and now she was telling me I should be happy with the changes he was making. Yes, in fact, I was happy—happy for him.

So, my coworker texted, "You want someone new or someone else you already know?" I replied, "I'm comfortable with our marriage counselor now." She said, "Call her." I responded, "I will later. I just want to cry, and be, and sleep right now." "Ok," she responded. And that's what I just did. My crying spells had become different. Before I would cry inconsolably, but now, my tears felt more like tears of release. Finally, in life I was beginning to allow myself to feel what I needed to feel. I don't even recall myself drifting off to sleep, but I slept for about two hours.

Ok, so you know how Freddy Krueger movies are, like the person is in real time, and then the person falls asleep, but it's not real time but it's real time? Well on this afternoon, my dream turned to real time with me being asleep in my bed. Now mind you, I don't normally sleep on my stomach anymore after pregnancy. I don't know why, but I can't sleep on my stomach—I have to be on my side or my back. What does that have to do with anything? Hell, I don't know! But anyway, I'm actually asleep on my stomach in real life, but in the Freddy Krueger dream I've funneled into, I'm also asleep on my stomach, and at this point I was feeling this presence of something, but I couldn't move! Like I could not literally move! And I felt like somebody was sitting on my husband's side of the bed. Now mind you, I'm on my stomach, my head is turned towards the left, which is facing his side of the bed, but the covers are up close to my face so I can't really see if anybody is there, but something is holding me, and I can't move. But you know how you feel like somebody is getting ready to touch you. But I couldn't move, and my heart was just pounding like, "SHIT!" And I was hoping and praying that it wasn't my husband, but then I was hoping and praying it was him, but still, I just could not move. And then finally, I was able to move in real life—and I looked, and nobody was there.

I was sweating profusely because it was just a dream, well, actually it was a nightmare. And I was like, what in the world is going on in my head? What is this all about? I was finally realizing that it was important for me to rest my mind. I am always on the go, I am always doing for others, I am always working, and I don't even take the time to take care of me and all that I am toiling with inside. Now back in the bed that I had not slept in since I don't know how long, my mind wandered.

The mind is a powerful thing. It is the control center for everything from emotions to actions. As I began to literally take steps in faith, I had to continuously work on my thoughts. I had become comfortable with the uncomfortable for so long, I had to learn to be still and be quiet before responding to anything. As a result of my emotions, I had to truly figure out that there were choices that I would have to make for me that must be based on facts and not my feelings. I had believed in my mind for so long that submitting meant that I had to do what my husband wanted, regardless of if I didn't honestly agree with him, because according to the Bible, isn't the man supposed to be the head of the house? As I began to truly study the Bible and depend on God to lead me, a lot was revealed to me about marriage. I realized that in the past I had not studied enough to truly grasp the expectations of both roles of husband and wife.

Most of my understanding came from what I saw and experienced through others' relationships, and a little knowledge came from premarital counseling, but my greatest understanding did not come until I truly sought the Lord for guidance as to whether or not I was justified to leave my marriage.

Through my daily devotionals and seeking passages associated with marriage, I began to realize many of the expectations and roles and responsibilities in a marriage, and the main one that continues to resonate with me is found in 1 Corinthians 11:3 (NIV), which says,

"But I want you to realize that the head of every man is Christ, and the head of the woman is man, and the head of Christ is God." In my situation, Christ was with us, but He was not in our marriage.

The spring was a season of tears, and as the old saying goes, April showers bring May flowers. They always seemed to form as I traveled to my counseling sessions. I came to realize that these tears were necessary. I had withheld so much over the years; things were finally coming out and I no longer carried the burden—these tears were cleansing. As I sat in counseling sessions during this season, I truly spoke my authentic feelings, withholding nothing. I was no longer receiving assistance from my previous counselor, but actually decided to see the counselor my husband sought out for us to use as a couple for my individual counseling as well. I felt this would be to my benefit since she knew the dynamics of us as a couple and our thoughts individually. I began to own my true feelings, not being afraid of another's reactions or responses, but speaking what I truly felt and owning every bit of it. I was truly able to communicate that I was at a point of no return, and I was ok with it. I was no longer putting off prioritizing me. I realized that I grew accustomed to being unhappy, and I was learning more and more how to change my mindset and seek happiness, but most importantly, joy. In my journal I wrote:

"Lord, I love you, and I just want to thank You. You have and continue to wrap your loving arms around me. I know I'm in your safety. You have given me signs that I need to accept at face value and begin to walk into my new season, for I AM WORTHY OF HAPPINESS! I AM WORTHY OF PEACE! I AM WORTHY OF CONTENTMENT! I AM STRONG enough to do it and live boldly. There are some things that I have been ignoring that will not allow me to live. I will work to release and relax without relapse. Lord, I just thank you for comfort."

During this time, I was also preparing to have knee surgery. I was staying with my parents most nights. They knew that something wasn't right, and I know they wanted to know what was going on, but they respected my simple response, "We have some things that we need to work out." Moreover, my father had recently had a pacemaker put in, and I in no way wanted to have him worried about me. As I was making plans for my knee surgery, I informed them that after my surgery I wanted to stay with them until I was able to literally get back on my feet. They were accepting of this, but I know they knew that was not the whole story. The night before my surgery I returned home so that I could be with my children. I wanted to reassure them that mommy was going to be ok.

The morning of my surgery my husband took me to the hospital, and my mom met us there. As I completed my paperwork, I specifically stated that I wanted to go back to my parents' house. My house was two-story, and I knew that I would not be able to manage going up and down the steps to sleep or access a full bathroom. My childhood home, on the other hand, was a ranch style home and I knew I would be able to maneuver in those confines better. My request was disregarded. As I slept in the car on the way home post-surgery, and I was awakened as my SUV pulled into the garage. Too drugged to fight, I was helped into the house, and made my way to the couch in the family room that would be my place of refuge until I could conquer steps. Drugged but coherent, I held off tears, but I lost that fight too. Tears flowed down my face, but when I was asked what was the matter, I blamed them on the surgery, because at that moment I realized that for the first time in many years, I accepted, and could feel that, my husband was working to truly assist me with love, compassion and tenderness. Now truly emotional, I am thankful for the pain medicine that allowed me to cry myself to sleep.

I was awakened by the sound of my children, the oldest shushing the others, as not to awaken me from my sleep. It brought tears to my eyes to see each of them and their faces of concern staring at me. I worked to give each one of them a gentle hug and kiss; them not knowing that their embraces were healing medicine for my heart. By this time, I was needing to get up and make my way to the bathroom. As I called my husband for assistance, a lump came in my throat and my eyes began to water. He worked to help me up, and we made our way to and from the destination. For the first time in a long time, I began to feel depressed with this current situation. I felt like I was in solitary confinement in this space. I had nowhere to retreat because of immobility. I could not help myself because I had to keep my leg elevated, and only felt like sleeping . . . and that is just what I did.

That night I found myself downstairs and all alone. So many thoughts were running through my head—confusion, frustration, loneliness, anxiety; I began to cry. I had to retreat mentally as I had learned to do during the last year. I searched for sermons on YouTube to calm my mind and focus. I came across a message that focused on I Corinthians 16:9 (KJV) which states, "For a great door and effectual is opened unto me, and there are many adversaries." At that moment, I realized that I must no longer fear taking my step of faith, and I must open the door at the appointed time. I had to stop all of the toiling and teetering back and forth. It had almost been a year, and I was still questioning whether or not I was doing the right thing. But truly reflecting in the moment, I realized that though I appreciated being cared for and loved (so it seemed) as he tried to assist me after surgery, there truly was nothing left for me to give. And that was yet another confirmation for me to remain forward, focused, and following in faith.

I finally made the transition to my parents' house once I was able to hobble around on my crutches. My dad was still recovering from his procedure, and I was able to persuade my husband that I wanted to stay with my parents so I could check on my dad and be in a house without steps so I could get to and from without much assistance. Waking up in my parents' home gave me peace. That morning I wrote in my journal:

"Lord, I thank you for another day which has not been seen before and will not be seen again. I don't know why I fear doing what my heart feels I should do. I do know what I need to do and I need to face it. I am scared. Scared of the unknown and what my children may think. However, you have not given me a spirit of fear, but of power and love, and of a sound mind (reference to 2 Timothy 1:7 [KJV]). Love—I love myself and others and this is one reason for what I'm doing. I have a sound mind; I'm not crazy and I don't make irrational decisions. Lord, please help me to understand and take my own advice that I don't have to justify anything to anybody. For you walk with me and talk with me along my life's journey. For you are with me every step of the way and walk before me, ordering my steps. Lord, thank you for continuing to strengthen me. I don't even give myself credit for my personal growth. I have not really stood on my own two feet in years, and I am grateful to be able to now. Lord, thank you for vision and clarity and the path and people along my journey. . . . "

After praying my prayer, I thought about the devotional I read for the morning, entitled "Strong and Confident" which focused on the following scripture. "This is my command—be strong and courageous! Do not be afraid or discouraged. For the Lord your God is with you wherever you go" (Joshua 1:9 [New Living Translation]). I also thought about the accompanying devotional which highlighted Romans 4:17 (KJV), "God . . . gives life to the dead and calls those things which do not exist as though they did." I was adamant that once I literally got back on my feet, I had to be strong and move forward to change my internal feeling of lifelessness to once again live the life that God has for me.

I realized that the restoration that God was ordaining would allow me to heal in many ways that would impact me in the coming months. This particular morning, God moved in a different way that would allow me to move forward but bring resolve to something I had been harboring for many years. Though I was a daddy's girl, my father and I did not always have a good relationship. I did work to honor him, but I had resentment built up over the years that caused tension between us. Long story short, I felt my dad stopped loving me when I was thirteen. When I reached junior high school, our relationship changed. He was not the pleasant and loving man I had once known. He seemed to have become bitter towards me, keeping me from doing anything I enjoyed outside of school and basketball. I did not realize what I could have done to make him treat me this way. When I asked him questions, as to why I wasn't permitted to do something, he would respond,

"Because I said so." And if I wanted to know something else, the most reaction I would get was a stare that could kill.

Over time, the resentment built up and in some ways I became rebellious. Years later when it came time for me to get married, I was relieved to no longer have to deal with the feeling of not being loved—another man would now fill that void. While I loved my husband, as a result of my feelings toward my father, I do feel that I looked at getting married as freedom from him—the man who was my first love, but who I no longer recognized, and to be quite honest, no longer respected.

When my husband asked my father for my hand in marriage, I was informed that my father said to him, "Remember that she can always come home." Who would have ever thought that I would have to possibly take him up on this promise?

This particular Sunday morning God moved in me to start a conversation with my father. I was learning that I had to become comfortable with the uncomfortable and that meant sometimes initiating and having those tough conversations that have been avoided over the years.

"Dad, I feel like you hated me when I was in junior high school. That hurt me and impacted my life." I had the strength to blurt the words out, but I couldn't hold back the tears. As I looked at my father, I am so thankful that he was sitting down, because I don't think he was prepared for such a conversation. My dad could be a very intimidating person, and his looks could mirror those characteristics, but this morning a humbling look I had never seen before was upon his face. He spoke in the softest tone I had ever heard him use, "I didn't know how to be a father to you." I definitely wasn't expecting that response, but I was still, and I listened. He went on to explain that he didn't have a father in his life, and that by being a male, he felt he could figure out how to raise my brother, but as far as how to treat a daughter, he was very unsure.

As a result of being a junior high school teacher, and all that he saw each and every day, he wanted to protect me so that I would not become a statistic and an embarrassment to him, so he felt the only way to prevent those things was to almost keep me in isolation. As the words came out, I was angry and frustrated, but as I looked at him and listened, I could feel his genuine concern. He apologized to me for the many lost years due to a lack of communication and understanding, but most importantly, he spoke open and honest to me of how proud he was of me that I didn't allow how he treated me to get in the way of me becoming a beautiful, successful, and loving individual.

As I sit and write about this encounter, I thank God for ordaining that day. I realize that everything happens for a reason, and God truly has a plan for our lives. Because of the challenges I was having in my marriage and staying with my parents, God saw fit for me to make amends with my father that day, healing my heart and preparing me for my unexpected loss of him a few months later.

CHAPTER 19

Point Of No Return

I noticed that through my prayers I focused a lot on praying for other individuals, and specifically praying continuously for my husband. However, I finally realized, the only person who I could really change and be responsible for their actions was me. At this point I began to pray very personal prayers—very specific prayers. Most of the focus for my prayers were for clear confirmation that I didn't have to even question.

We had not had much discussion, but I needed to know if any leads had been made for my husband to find a place of his own. When we spoke about separating, he said he would find a place. The summer was approaching, and the kids would be getting out of school soon, and this would be the most ideal time to begin a transition, but not surprisingly, he had no leads. This frustrated me. I could not understand what could be preventing him from finding a place to live, but then I had to remind myself of his track record with me and following through. So, I asked if I should look for a place or if he would do so, and he confirmed he would. In the interim I stated that we would at this point have to split all bills 50/50. I had truly grown tired and weary of everything, but this would honestly be the last try at seeing if we could truly work together for a common goal.

I spelled out all of the monthly bills that I had been responsible for and he provided the same for me. We agreed that he would give the money to me since most of the bills were in my name and I had set up autopay on most accounts. The first of June arrived, and based upon our discussion I moved forward with paying bills as I normally did, with the expectancy that he would provide me with his half for the month. Days passed and nothing was said, and finally one day he provided me with a check, but it was not for the amount we had agreed upon. I asked where was the rest and his response was that he didn't have it. I grew angry and asked how he could agree upon paying half if he knew he couldn't. I honestly don't remember his response, but I do know that my thought process was that all he had to do was be honest with me about what he could and could not do. I had been more than accommodating over the years, and even during this time period after stating we needed to separate. I realized at this point I had to ensure that I was not sending any mixed signals to him that I would be remaining in this marriage. Unfortunately, as a result of my standing up for myself, speaking exactly what I felt and being honest with him, it seemed to be taken as I was being mean. I was at the point of no return, and I knew that I could not do anything about his perspective, but I could do something about me and my peace.

With the month of July came a new fiscal year and mindset for me. Over the course of my marriage, my finances had taken a hit; I could not allow this to discourage me from moving forward. At the time I was reading *The Circle Maker* by Mark Batterson. This book focused on praying circles around your biggest dreams and greatest fears. It taught me the true power of a single prayer, and just like circling the walls of Jericho, I was persistent with certain prayers that would assist me with walking into my new season. Not only did the book assist me, but I was reminded of the affirmations that I had written with my life coach. One included the following: "I am living a prosperous and financially healthy lifestyle with blessings to pay my tithes and the means to enjoy the tangible things in life." Every day I spoke my affirmations and always this one first. I also started a financial journal and spoke abundance over my situation; however, even with all of this, I began to question whether or not I could actually make it on my own. Even though I tracked every bill, accounted for possible miscellaneous occurrences, I still had doubts in my mind. Throughout this entire book I have worked to avoid talking about the enemy, because I did not want to give him any credit, but I learned during the last few weeks before I took my step in faith, he would be out to do all he could to keep me bound. Yet through prayer and faith, everything began to work in my favor.

As I sat in the office area of the house one Saturday morning, I stared into space and tears began to roll down my face as I thought to myself, *What does it profit a man to gain the whole wide world and lose his own soul?* Again, the devil was trying to get into my mind. I looked around and had the family, the home, the cars—things that many people wished they had and the exact things that I dreamed about at one time in life. However, even though I had these things, my soul was in recovery as God was working to restore my joy. At that moment I decided I could no longer be worried about what other people may think or say, for they do not know my story, they have not walked in my shoes, and I am only responsible for me and my happiness. As I said that to myself, I thought again of the time when my husband told me that he was not responsible for my happiness. When he said that initially, I couldn't understand it. My thought process was that my husband would pour into me and do things with and for me to create happiness. Now, I could appreciate what he was saying. I truly am responsible for my own happiness, but most importantly I am seeking the joy that the world can't give to me.

If my daily devotionals weren't speaking to me before, they were taking me by the hand and walking me into my new season each day. "Call to me and I will answer you. I'll tell you marvelous and wondrous things that you could never figure out on your own" (Jeremiah 33:3 [NIV]). After reading this in the *3-Minute Devotions for Women* I knew that I could no longer come up with my own plan, I needed to take everything to God in prayer and meditation and trust Him. "Peace I leave with you; my peace I give to you. I do not give to you as the world gives. Do not let your hearts be troubled and do not be afraid" (John 14:27 [NIV]). Day after day after day I received clear scripture with answers to my fears and concerns. I was unsure as to when I was to literally walk into my new life, but I knew a clear sign would come . . . and then it happened.

On the morning of August 3rd, I opened up my book, *Daily Readings from the Power of I Am*, and the devotional for the day was entitled "Steps of Faith." I had talked about taking the initial step, but mentally, I didn't think I was truly prepared, so I ignored the devotional and all that it spoke to that aligned with me. Then the next day, I read the devotional "Try It" and the scripture was from Malachi 3:10 (NLT), "I will pour out a blessing so great you won't have enough room to take it in! Try it! Put me to the test." This confident individual that I was becoming began to retreat and second guess everything that I was reading daily. Though God was providing me with the answers, I was still in disbelief that I could hear him so clearly. He was even providing the reassurance financially. "They will not be disgraced in hard times and even in famine they will have more than enough" (Psalm 37:19 [NLT]). A year to the date was approaching as to when I initially told my husband we needed to separate. Though I worked to pay most of the bills in the home, I still questioned whether or not I could survive on my own. I didn't have confidence because I had also allowed my credit to take a turn for the worse during my marriage. I was coming up with every excuse there was as to why maybe I should stay, yet I knew there was nothing left for me to give, and I would definitely stay because that is what was expected of me and not what was in my heart.

Each day was the same; another verse of provision— "And God will generously provide all you need. Then you will always have everything you need and plenty left over to share with others." (2 Corinthians 9:8 [NIV]). I tried to convince myself that this devotional by Joel Osteen just happened to have scriptures that by chance aligned with all the thoughts and prayers I had at the time. Then I received my gut punch after receiving subtle signs from God. Before I prepared for church one Sunday, I hesitantly opened up my morning read and looked at the title: "Be on Purpose." The scripture read, "Be careful then how you live, not as unwise people but as wise, making the most of the time. (Ephesians 5:15-16 [New Revised Standard Version]). And if this wasn't enough, my second devotional selection from my other book highlighted I Chronicles 22:18 (KJV), "Is not the Lord your God with you . . .?" Then I wrote my prayer for the morning:

"Lord, you are always with me. Let me know that getting my own place is the right thing to do. Lord, I am not happy. I have struggled for years, and it is not fair to myself, my husband, nor the kids to be like this and feeling the way I do in an unhealthy environment. I am very uncomfortable, but You said you will be with me, and I am trusting in Your word and Your way. Help me to be bold, steadfast, and unmovable always abounding in Your work. Comfort my children so that they know this decision is not because of them. Be with me and my husband to help us see what is best for us moving forward. Lord, I need peace in my mind, peace in my heart, and peace in my spirit. Amen."

I knew this Sunday morning I would receive a word at church that would speak directly to me; and my pastor did not disappoint. This particular morning, I took my journal to church to capture the message; usually I return home to write down the notes I had taken from the sermon on my bulletin. My ears perked up as Pastor Jones got into the sermon. I'll paraphrase his message:

"We're not enjoying life because we're living in anxiety and fear. So often we get caught up in how people look. You can be pretty but if you have a cold heart, there is nothing pretty about you. The question isn't a new question—if you want to see the kingdom of God—you shouldn't have to drag someone into the church . . . So often we get caught up in what we see, but what do people see in a church when they see you? The kingdom of God is in your midst . . . We live in a world where we have anxiety, etc. Just because you pray doesn't mean it's going to be as we want it. It is what it is but if You believe God is in control, how dare you have anxiety and allow yourself to feel down . . . How dare you allow yourself to live with anxiety and depression when it's temporary. And some things are the way they are because we haven't done what we need to do . . . We've got to be faithful—look beyond the rhetoric of the moment."

"For I know the plans I have for you," declares the LORD, "plans to prosper you and not to harm you, plans to give you hope and a future" (Jeremiah 29:11 [NIV]). God has a plan for you—you still have not arrived. You don't know it all . . . "And we know that all things work together for good to them that love God, to them who are the called according to his purpose" (Romans 8:28 [KJV]). "If God is for you, who can be against you?" (Romans 8:31 [NLT]).

At this point I am in tears and unable to truly capture anything else. My tears were tears of relief. I didn't know Joel Osteen and refused to accept what was being revealed through his book, but I did know my pastor, and he was the shepherd who has fed me the word since I was five years old. He was also the man who considered me his daughter. He was the one that I would call on as I got older and didn't feel comfortable speaking to my own father about matters. He was also the one who conducted both premarital counseling and individual counseling sessions with me. There was no denying that God had given him this message specifically for me (and of course others) at this time; only God's timing is so perfect.

CHAPTER 20

I Surrender All

The next month of my life would be one that was focused on the scripture found in Psalms 46:10 (KJV), "Be still, and know that I am God." As I was scrolling social media, I ran across a post that quoted Becca Lee:
"If you seek peace, be still
If you seek wisdom, be silent.
If you seek love, be yourself."

I did just that. There was no longer doubt in my mind that God had a purpose and plan for my life. There was no longer doubt in my mind that He would order my steps. There was no longer doubt in my mind that I could move forward, while focused, and following in faith. Almost a month to the day that I received the message from my pastor, I decided to find myself a new home. I knew through prayer and patience He would lead me to my new beginning. I can recount this time as if it happened yesterday as I reflect on a few of my journal entries. That day I wrote in my journal:

"Lord, thank You for this day in September . . . Lord, I continuously thank you for my children, and especially my little girl. I thank you for entrusting me with the honor of being her mother. What a great responsibility?! I do not take it for granted. I thank You for the experience I had with my mother, and I pray that You allow me to use it and enhance it with the knowledge and understanding I have and continue to gain as a woman over the years to help her learn, grow, develop, and come into her own. Lord, continue to work in and on me as I make decisions in my life that impact not only me, but others around me, and particularly my daughter as she grows and develops. May I remain faithful, forward, focused, and following You and Your word. Bless the plans and activities you set forth for me to complete on this day. I love you, Lord. Amen."

The next Sunday after church service I wasn't going to speak to my pastor, but I decided to anyway. When I spoke to him, I told him I needed to meet with him. He reminded me that I had his number. I said that I needed to speak about some personal and professional things. He stated to me, again referencing the sermon he had just preached about storms, "When you stand still and go through your storm, the hardest step is to walk away but there comes a time when you have to." I am sure you can imagine how I felt in that very moment. I was just about faint, standing in the front of the church, but I gathered up enough strength to walk away and make it to my car. I couldn't drive home at the moment, because I needed to get myself together. I decided to call my friend, Michelle. My devotional that morning focused on being at peace because God is my refuge, and pastor had just spoken about peace in the storm. I had to confide all of this in her and hear her response. She had truly become my prayer partner and circle maker friend, and I just needed some support in order to grasp yet again what I believed was confirmation from above.

As I drove home, I spent time with her talking about the details of the sermon and how it was aligned with my life right now. When I hung up the phone with Michelle, Marvin Sapp's song, "Close" was playing as I entered the garage to my home of almost thirteen years. I took this as yet another sign that my breakthrough was near. Later that week, I began to search for a new home. I prayed to God like never before and wrote in my journal:

"Lord, be with me and be my strength. You will never leave me nor forsake me. You will not put more on me than I can bear. Lord, allow me to keep my eyes stayed on Thee. May I remain forward, focused, and following You. Give me words to speak or hold my tongue so that I do not say anything out of spite. Lord, help me to find a place in close proximity and at the right price that will allow me to be able to take care of my new household and help with the other house so that we don't lose it. Guide me oh, Thy Great Jehovah.

Lord, I put this home search in Your hands. Lord, please allow me to find a place that is suitable for me and my children. Lord, let me be fiscally responsible with my choice. Lord, if it is best for me to rent an apartment in order to care for my children, pay bills and be fiscally responsible, show me the way. Lord, I thank you for this peaceful feeling I have right now after the conversation about separating. This was definitely unexpected. I thought I would be crying inconsolably, but I am stronger and more confident in me. Lord, please allow me to stay strong and rest. May I not make any hasty decisions but remain with a calm mind. In Jesus' name. Amen."

In a notebook I wrote at the top of the page, "Lord be with me, and be my strength." There were nine listings that I found that met the criteria that I prayed about, and looking back now, I realize that everything God truly ordains, because the one that He had for me was one of them that had been listed.

CHAPTER 21

New Beginnings, New Opportunities, New Blessings, & New Mercies

he next morning, I awakened and began my normal routine; however, on this particular morning I did not have to get up as early because it was a teacher workday for my husband and the kids. There was a different air about me this morning, and the daily devotional from Joel Osteen spoke to it. The scripture for the message spoke about grace, and how God gives us more grace. In James 4:6 I read, "God opposes the proud but shows favor to the humble." Then the *3-Minute Devotions for Women* reading spoke about "Microwave Faith" and referenced Hebrews 6:15, "And so, after waiting patiently, Abraham received what was promised." I received all of this in the name of Jesus as I prepared for the day. God had given me grace and I knew that He would keep His promise and provide me a home for a new beginning.

As I left the neighborhood headed to work, I realized that I was ahead of schedule, so I decided to just look nearby to see if there may have been some houses that were on the market but didn't appear for some reason in my search. I checked in a nearby neighborhood that I had forgotten about and found a couple of houses with a rental sign in the yard. The company allowed you to access the homes by just calling a number and receiving an access code. When I called the number posted, I was informed that the particular home I wanted to view was actually being removed from the system because a lease agreement had been signed. However, the agent informed me that there were other homes in the vicinity, which were comparable to the one I was inquiring about. Because I was driving and couldn't take down any notes, the agent took my personal information, what I was looking for in a rental, and stated she would send me information about other properties that fit the criteria.

On my drive into work, I called my friend, Michelle, as I usually did, and we had conversations about our devotionals for the morning. I then began to tell her about how I had contacted a property management group about some rental properties in the area. Before I could get to work, I received the notifications in reference to a few homes. As I transitioned into my office, I knew I would not have time to check the listings because I had a jam packed schedule. So, as I worked at my desk, my dear friend reached out to the agent to inquire about one particular home that stood out to me. As we sat on the phone together, she connected me through a conference call. With my phone muted, I listened as she took the lead to set up a possible viewing of the home. Within minutes, I was scheduled to view the home during my lunch break. I was actually caught off guard; I wasn't expecting for the viewing to be scheduled until the evening or another day.

As I put the address in my navigation system, I realized that this home was in the neighborhood beside my children's school. As I entered the neighborhood, I began to see signs that this was most likely going to be my next home. One of the streets was named Laura Michelle—how ironic. At the time, I was on the phone with my friend Michelle, who has been by my side along this journey. As I pulled up to the home my heart began to beat rapidly in excitement. I was finally feeling good about taking a step forward. As I opened the door, I knew that this would be the home. I walked around and it had everything that I was looking for, and specifically, enough rooms for each of my children to have their own space. My excitement faded though as I began to think about how I would be approved for this home.

Starting over truly meant starting over. I needed to rebuild not only myself, but my credit, which I allowed to be damaged. As I drove back to work, I started thinking about how I worked to do what my husband wanted to in the marriage by letting him decide how we would go about paying bills; everything for the most part was in my name. The bills that I was responsible for each month were paid on time, but I could not say that for the others. We encountered some hard times in the marriage where he was unemployed, and some things didn't get paid or would be delinquent. On top of our household bills, I had college loans (and part of them were a result of me taking out more than I needed for tuition to help when my husband didn't have income coming in), and I was adamant about paying them, but he would say, we'll get them paid, and pay only partial or make no payment at all. As much as I could request a forbearance or deferment I would, but eventually, I just gave up. With the growth of our family, there were medical bills and childcare that made me feel like we were drowning. We were living beyond our means, and I would try to work with him and talk about this, but it didn't seem to be a problem for him.

My excitement about the home was taken over with frustration of all that I had allowed. As I returned to work and walked into my building to prepare for my next meeting, I felt defeated before my search for a place had truly begun. As I sat down at my desk my eyes focused on the mustard seed that was taped to my computer. This seed had been on my computer since 2013 when God spoke to me in my office and I heard him clearly say, "Trust Me" in reference to a professional decision I had to make. I immediately began to pray about the situation and asked that God's will be done. Over this past year, I was growing more and more confident in praying and truly *letting go and letting God*.

The next day, before I headed to work, I decided to drive by the home I was interested in. I was moved to circle the house seven times and pray about it, as I learned that many believers in Christ had done in the book *The Circle Maker*. I knew that all things were in God's hands and His will would be done.

As I sat in a meeting, I received an email notification on my phone that asked me to complete a survey about my visit to the rental property. To pass the time in the meeting, I pulled up my personal email account and completed the survey. After completing it, I received another communication with information about applying for the property. I didn't take a minute to think about it. I filled out the application and said to myself, the worst response that I can receive is a no. After completing the application and uploading the appropriate documents, which to my surprise I had access to while in my office, I received a confirmation email that my application had been received and would be reviewed. I had convinced myself that there was no way I would qualify for the home due to debt and my credit score, so I went on with work and didn't think anything more about it. When I returned to my office at the end of the day, I realized that my personal email was still open on my computer, and I opened it to receive confirmation that I had been approved!

CHAPTER 22

Speak Into Existence

At this point in life, I was truly walking into a new season. From being approved for the rental property that I desired to serving as a speaker for a women's empowerment conference, Ignite Your Passion, founded by my dear friend Alisha, I was beginning to truly understand the importance of speaking into existence your goals and aspirations and stepping out in faith to achieve them. Not only did I work to speak things into existence, I realized that it was time to have a conversation with my parents about what was taking place in my life.

I decided to visit my parents after my speaking engagement. It just so happened that my dad had just been released from the hospital and my brother was transporting him back home. My mother had been in attendance at the conference to hear me speak, and so we all arrived at my childhood home around the same time. Once I determined my dad was in good spirits, I felt that time was better than any other to engage in this conversation. I began telling my parents about my spiritual journey since December 22, 2017, and surprisingly, my dad stated he knew and could see and feel the change. For those who don't know, we believe my dad did have some kind of special sense that allowed him to prophesy and predict certain things. I knew he may have been telling the truth because he was very calm and not interruptive as I spoke. As I finished telling them about my spiritual walk, I proceeded to speak about how I had been struggling in my marriage for many years.

Somewhat shocked, my dad said, "Why didn't you tell us before now?" I reminded them that when they gave my hand away in marriage, I was to cleave to my husband, and not them. I added that if I would have told them some of the things I had experienced, my dad (and brother) probably would have killed my husband. They laughed a little bit, but my face and body language showed my seriousness.

I then began to explain that I had decided to move out, and my mind was made up. I reminded them of who I was and the fact that I do not make irrational decisions, and I analyze everything I do. However, when I make my mind up about something, there is nothing anyone can say or do to change it. My parents knew I was serious, and as they have always done in my life, they supported me with my decision and told me that they would help me in any way that I needed. Though I wasn't worried about their support, it was relieving to finally tell them what was really going on in my life. We were a close-knit family, and it killed me to keep things from them.

I proceeded to inform them that I was approved for a rental home, and I may need their assistance financially to make the move. As with everything else in my life, my dad immediately asked how much I needed. I told him I appreciated his gesture, but I wanted to see what I could manage first before getting their assistance. As expected, their main concern was the kids—how was this going to impact them? I knew as grandparents, but especially as parents, they wanted to ensure the kids would be ok. I had to remind them, as my life coach instilled in me, I can't be good and healthy for them if I am not taking care of myself.

That evening I returned home to love on my children. After I put them to bed and got settled into my daughter's room, which is where I slept when I was in our house, I opened up my YouTube app to find a devotional and on my screen was T.D. Jakes and his sermon "When to Move On." He talked about how the eagle sits and waits to see if an egg is going to hatch but realizes that sometimes some things refuse to grow. He continued to speak about how the hardest thing in work, life, relationships, etc. is knowing when to give up. What he said next resonated with me and my current situation, "When is it a matter of more faith?" He continued, "There is a point when the mother gives up when she compromises her future, her destiny, by laying on her dead history she will miss the chance to birth again. There is nothing like knowing when to move on. I said to myself, *Lord, I'm listening*.

The next morning when I rose, I was excited to see what the devotional for the day would focus on; I never looked ahead. This morning it was entitled "Endure till the End." Joel Osteen referenced one of my favorite verses, Ecclesiastes 9:11, ". . . the race is not to the swift or the battle to the strong . . ." This gave me comfort in knowing that I had not been quick to come up with the decision to move on, but I had sought ways to try to mend what was broken inside of me, and I had prayed continuously for the answer, and I had endured what God had planned at this point in my life. I was prepared to take bold steps of faith to do what He would have me to do. I was truly learning to trust Him, even though it was not easy. For the first time in years, I was excited about all that was in store.

The next morning was filled with excitement for me, as it was the day that my life forever changed ten years before; I became a mom to my oldest son. I looked forward to the day ahead because it was one of the few days, he would be happy to see his mom show up at lunch because I would have birthday treats to share with his friends. I also realized this would probably be the last time we would share in such a celebration at school, because he would be a middle schooler next year. With all of the excitement about this big day, I had to also focus on the fact that I would have 24 hours to sign the least for the home that I prayed about or risk forfeiting it to another resident. After speaking with my parents and the confirmations I received, I knew that I would have to have the official conversation with my husband.

As I prepared to sign the lease that morning, I prayed the following prayer:

"Lord, I come to you now as humbly as I know how, thanking you for what you've done and continue to do in my life. Lord, be with me and help me have the confidence to move forward in faith, focused, and following You. May the work I do allow me to maintain all responsibilities for my home, me, and my children. Thank you for supportive parents to help me with the deposit. I step out in faith right now and sign the lease for my new home as I get my life back and restore the joy. I thank You. I love You. I trust You. Amen."

At 10:31 a.m. I signed the lease electronically and clicked submit. Not to overshadow the day of celebration for our son, I decided the conversation with my husband would not take place until the next day. Both devotionals I read for the day helped to prepare me mentally. One entitled "The Victory Given," which Osteen focused on 1 Corinthians 15:57 stated, "But thanks be to God! He gives us the victory through our Lord Jesus Christ." Also, "Answered Prayer" from the *3-Minute Devotions for Women,* which referenced Psalms 37:4 English Standard Version, "Delight yourself in the Lord; and He will give you the desires of your heart." I had asked God to show me what to do and order my steps, and now he was giving me the desires of my heart, though bittersweet. I chose myself and had to do what was necessary for me to love myself again and live again in my truth and authentically. This was, in fact, a victory won.

Not only was this a victory won, but I was truly beginning to feel like this journey was bigger than me. I didn't know why, and I didn't know how it would make an impact, but as with everything else, I would remain forward, focused, and following in faith to see. As I prepared to pray for this morning, instead of an actual prayer, the words to "Give Us This Day", as sung by Whitney Houston, came to me and I wrote it instead of my own prayer.

I continued to thank God for yet another day—one not seen before and never to be seen again. I thanked Him for all that He had done and was doing in my life. That morning I really didn't have a lot on my heart as I felt that I was freeing myself. I was so thankful for this growth and transformation.

That evening would be the evening that I would communicate to my husband that I had found a place and I would be moving out. I can recall that evening so vividly. I had taken my daughter to dance as I had each Tuesday, and when I returned to the house, the pressure from anxiety fell upon me. I loved the fact that I was coming home to my children, but I dreaded the fact of everything else within the home. I was very quiet that evening, mumbling only a "Hey." as I entered the bedroom to place my shoes in the closet and sit on the bed for a little while before getting everyone ready for the night.

For the first time in a while, I sat on my side of the bed. The television was on and I was staring at it, but I wasn't watching it. I was thinking to myself; *I have to do this. I can't take it anymore.* I guess my look and body language showed that too, because my husband said, "You look like something is wrong." I said, "It is." He said, "What is it?" I said, "I can't say in front of the kids." So, he asked the children to go to their rooms so we could talk. When all three left, a complete calmness came over me. I turned my head to the right to face him, and I finally spoke and said, "I can't do this anymore. Have you found a place?" As usual, he was hesitant with his response. Though it shouldn't have, this question seemed to have caught him off guard. He responded, "Nah, I haven't." I said, "Well I have been looking for places and I will move. I have tried to give you opportunities to find a place, and I have stayed in this house in misery, but I just can't do it anymore." I asked him, "Can you afford to stay here and keep the bills up so we don't lose the house?" With frustration he responded, "It will be hard, but I will make it happen." I said, "Are you sure, because I will not be able to support two houses." Though he was not a man of many words or emotions, I could feel tension, but I could not let that (as it had in the past) prevent me from seeing this conversation through. He repeated, "Like I said, it will be hard, but I will make it happen."

I responded, "Ok. I think this is best for us. I believe that separation will give us time to see if we can work things out. We continue to live like roommates and have for a long time." I continued, "Separation may allow us time apart to see what the other person brings to the table, and absence may actually make the heart grow fonder." He was quick to respond, "I don't believe that!" I replied, "I can't control how you feel; I can only speak on what I believe."

He followed up with, "Well, you gotta tell the kids!" as if that was going to hinder me. I responded, "Ok." He immediately yelled to the kids to come to our room. I will not lie, I did feel like this was going to be as difficult as it was initiating the conversation with him, but as I had just done, I asked the Lord to be with me.

When the kids entered, all I could see was innocence. They had not been asked to come into this world. That was a decision made by the two of us. We were responsible for them and their well-being. As a mother, I continued to focus on the fact that in order for me to be good for them I had to be good for myself. I began to craft the conversation in a way that I hoped at least a ten-year-old and a seven-year-old would be able to understand, if not a three-year-old. As I began to engage in conversation with the children, I could feel my husband's eyes look on. I said to them, "You all know that mommy and daddy love you so very much. More than anything in this world, right?" They responded in affirmation, and I continued. "Well, as I said before, mommy and daddy are not good friends right now, and that has nothing to do with you all. So mommy has decided that she is going to move into another house."

Before I could finish, my son said, "Does that mean we will have two houses?" I responded, "Yes." My daughter responded, "So does that mean you will be like Courtney's mom and dad." Kids are definitely smarter and more resilient than we give them credit for in difficult situations. I responded, "Yes." Though my husband and I were both expecting different responses, and not necessarily responses as lighthearted as these, the kids from my perspective seemed to receive it and understand it. I asked them if they had any questions, and they confirmed they didn't. So, I told them they needed to get ready for bed and I would check on them.

To be quite honest, I don't remember much of the conversation that may have taken place after that, but I do know that I found comfort in knowing that I had spoken my peace and my children's responses gave me confidence that things would be alright.

CHAPTER 23

It's Your Time

T hrough the next morning's devotionals, the scripture reminded me, "I can do all things through Him who strengthens and empowers me" (Philippians 4:13 Amplified Bible). I was also reminded of the promise of God in Leviticus 18:2-3 Amplified Bible, "I am the Lord your God, your God. You shall not do what is done in the land of Egypt where you lived, and you shall not do what is done in the land of Canaan where I'm bringing you." Yesterday I had taken yet another bold step in faith only a little over a year from the time that I first spoke words of separation to my husband. I knew that God was with me and would direct me every step of the way on my new path, but I could not do what I had done and could no longer live as I had. He was giving me a new opportunity to live again. Moreover, I could not expect to do what others may have done or expect for me to do along my journey ahead, but I can look to Him for guidance. As I write this chapter, I looked back in my journal at the prayer that I wrote for this particular morning and the one thing that sticks out to me is the fact that even after all that I have been through, and the reality of separation, I continuously kept my husband lifted in prayer each and every day.

Though I had signed the lease agreement, I still had to submit the security deposit and provide evidence of renter's insurance in order to complete all contractual obligations. Additionally, I had to figure out what to do about the utilities. During my lunch break, I visited my parents and let them know that I had communicated with my husband that I would be moving out. They asked me how they could assist. I informed them I may need help with the deposit, and as a result of my husband not paying utilities on time that were all in my name, I was sure I would have to put security deposits down on all of the requests at the new residence. My dad responded, "You know we are going to help you. Your momma can go to the bank and transfer the money into your account for the deposit. As far as the utilities were concerned, he told my mother, "Just give her the card." He said to me, "Just do what you need to do. You owe us anyway." My dad had a terrible time trying to joke at a time that most of us considered serious, but I knew he had no intention of hurting my feelings. I humbly thanked them and returned to work.

That Thursday, before heading to work, I stopped by the property management company and submitted my security deposit. Everything seemed to be going quicker than I expected. I headed to work and again I visited my parents' house during lunch. I worked in haste to make things happen associated with the utilities. However, before I even made the first call I had to pray. I had gotten frustrated thinking about the many times I had asked my husband to put the utilities in his name. Before we got married, I had purchased my own home, and everything was in my name. Once we got married and moved to the current house, the utilities were just transferred. During that transition I found out that he had not been paying them on time, and deposits had to be put down again. Throughout the marriage I asked him to put them in his name, but he never did. As a result, now I was suffering once again as a consequence of his delinquency and disregard of my pleas. Reflecting now on the scripture referenced in that morning's devotional from John 14:1 (NIV), "Do not let your hearts be troubled. You believe in God; believe also in me." I realized at that point, I allowed a lot of things to take place in the past that I shouldn't have and I had to prepare to face them and work to rebuild.

That weekend would be a bittersweet weekend. Though there was tension among us, my husband and I worked to celebrate my son's birthday with his friends and siblings at Carowinds on Saturday. I truly believe we both had the desire to work together for their benefit and to show them that even though we may not get along, our love and support for them remained.

On Sunday, as usual before preparing for church, I went through my daily ritual of giving at least the first hour of my morning to God. This morning, the verse from *3-Minute Devotions for Women* stated, "The prayer of the righteous is powerful and effective" (James 5:16 [NRSV]). I was a walking billboard and could testify to its truth and I prayed:

"Lord, I thank You for last night's rest. It was necessary and I feel much better. I know you are allowing me to enter into a new season. As you have in the past, walk before me and order my steps. May I walk in confidence. May my new home be a place of peace and serenity. Lord, I thank You for supporting me in one of the biggest steps in my life. Please keep me in perfect peace with my mind stayed on Thee. For you know the plans You have for me . . . Lord bless and keep my family and friends. Show them Your favor and who you are. May today be the first day of the best days of my life. I claim and count it done. In Jesus' name. Amen."

This morning I decided to attend 7:30 a.m. service at church, expecting to receive a word from my pastor. However, the message was delivered from another minister, Reverend Reginald Blackmon, but as through my experience, the message, "Ten Keys to the Kingdom," was right on time. He focused on three keys in his message: faith, prayer, and calling on the name of Jesus. He reminded us that there is a source within us to get what we need to enhance the quality of our lives. When Paul wrote Ephesians, he was in prison, but he wanted people to know that God had mapped out their destination. He then began to speak on each of the three keys. I will paraphrase what he shared with us,

"Faith . . . understanding whatever we go through, God is always there and waiting on us to get there. Sometimes we wake up in our prayer life and want instant results. When we call on Him he will work it out by and by if we just wait on Him. Prayer...our communication with God; our fellowship with God, which deepens with consistency...He will prepare a table in the presence of your enemies . . . Call on His Name . . . Discipline and obedience are needed to get a prayer through, and the ability to call on the name of Jesus . . . He will make a way out of no way. There is nothing like the name of Jesus."

After that service I decided it was time. As I left the sanctuary with my mother and her best friend, I invited them to see where I would be living. As we traveled along the way, I began to speak to them about the message and how it aligned with me and the new journey I was about to begin. When we drove into the driveway it really felt like I was coming home. I gave them a tour of the inside and they agreed it was nice. When my mother and I were one-on-one, she spoke and said that she was proud of me. That meant more to me than she would ever know.

That evening after putting my children to bed and preparing to head to my parents' house as usual, I decided it was my time to move in, as I had already secured the keys. At first, I wanted to wait until I had furniture and everything in place for my children, but my heart and mind felt differently—it was time. I departed from the place I had called home for thirteen years and drove to my new residence. With only a blowup mattress, pillow, and a quilt my mother made me, I turned the key to my front door and walked into my new season.

As I sat in my room alone, I entered into my closet to pray. All I can remember is sitting in silence for a period of time on my knees. Warm tears flowed down my face as I began to think about all that I had been through and what was to come, yet there was a peace over me—a calmness—a comfort in knowing that I was choosing me and walking by faith and not by sight. After completing my prayer, I prepared for bed. That night, for the first night in many years, I slept with no worries, no pain, no anxiety, no frustration—I was at peace in my peaceful palace.

The next morning, I traveled to my old house to awake the kids and prepare them for the day. As I sat on the couch in the old family room after my first night in my new home, I worked on my devotional. My husband had left, and I had time before awakening the kids to get them ready for school. The reading for this morning was entitled, "In the Furnace." Joel Osteen's message focused on the scripture from Isaiah 48:10, "See, I have refined you, though not as silver; I have tested you in the furnace of affliction." As I thought to myself about all that I had been through, God truly tested me and my faith. I never would have thought in a million years I would be where I was at this time—on the path to divorce. My intention for moving out was to determine if space would allow the two of us to see where we may have taken the other person for granted, and also give us time to work on ourselves. I also prayed that it would be a time for us to work to rebuild what had been broken. But my husband said if I moved out that would be it. Choices--we all have to make them and live with the consequences, whether good or bad. So, at this time in my life, I chose me and chose to live in the moment with no regrets, and remain forward focused, and following in faith to see what God had planned for me.

EPILOGUE

"Untitled"
You just might believe
Delusional disguised reprieves
Heart embroidered with camouflaged words
To convince you that you're a caged bird
With clipped wings
That's an invalid reason to not dream
You see . . . the mind dictates
What the brain emulates
So welcome healing modifications
Embrace sanguine expectations
Become reacquainted with your right to rebel
Now is time to empower yourself.
~Dr. Karen D. Morgan

November 9, 2020

Two years ago, on this day I read *God's Way* from *The Daily Readings* from *The Power of I Am* by Joel Osteen, not realizing then where God would lead me. That same morning, I read "Not Now God" from *3-Minute Devotions for Women.* In my journal I captured the following scripture from that text: "The end of a matter is better than its beginning, and patience is better than pride" (Ecclesiastes 7:8). I never would have imagined two years ago that I would feel so loved and empowered after experiencing four of the five most stressful events in life simultaneously: separation leading to divorce, moving out of my home, the death of my father, and being diagnosed with a medical condition—but EVERYTHING GOD ORDAINS (E.G.O.).

As I reflect now, I'm glad I realized that when I chose God's way for my life, there would be no place for my little ego, but my life would be led my big E.G.O. In the same manner, the scripture above sums up my JOurneY over the course of two years, and like the lyrics of a song that stayed on repeat, *Your Latter Will be Greater*; I never would have imagined. The end of my marriage was actually the beginning of my REstoration. I am a walking testimony that you have to go T.H.R.O.U.G.H. (Trials, Hurts, Regrets, Obstacles, Uncertainty, Guilt, Heartbreak) for your BREAKTHROUGH.

As I continue to read the journal entry for this day, I said:

"Lord, You are showing me more and more of Your favor for me. You are showing me more and more the true me. I almost said new me, but everything was always in me. I just had to experience what you had in store for me in order to be REstored. I am so grateful for this journey. I am seeing more and more of what I am capable of and understand with patience and being still and quiet, You will lead me and guide me.

Here I am today, living my latter and reaping the harvest God promised me. A month ago, I was promoted to Associate Vice President for Academic Affairs. This position didn't even exist, but in the same way that God opens and closes doors—He can create doors. What began as a way for me to share my journey through the unknown has now evolved into a ministry, My Big E.G.O. Life, LLC., a platform used to share my life experiences ordained by God and to assist others with experiencing a transformation of mind, body, and soul. Not only have I transformed spiritually, but I have transformed physically, dropping over 30 pounds and three dress sizes. Financially—with a focus on giving of my tithes first, I have paid off all of my debt except for my college loans (and I'm believing my Ephesians 3:20 blessing is on the way to cancel them out). I never would have imagined that I would experience labor again, but God saw fit for me to birth this book. Most importantly, though, I have experienced true love—love I only dreamed about, because now I am truly living . . . but that's a whole other story.

Made in the USA
Columbia, SC
18 November 2021

49228307R00076